INDEX TO DEPARTMENTS

IMPORTANCE OF GOOD COOKING

HEALTHFUL cookery is not receiving the attention which its importance demands. Although we are living at a time when eating and drinking are carried to excess, and when elaborate bills of fare are frequently placed before us, yet plain, simple, and healthful cookery occupies but a comparatively small place in the culinary world to-day.

Good food is of primary importance. We live upon what we eat. It is not sufficient, however, merely to select good food. To be well digested and thoroughly assimilated the food must be properly prepared. The best food may be spoiled in cooking. The kind of food upon which we live, and the manner in which it is prepared, determines largely our physical well-being, and consequently much of our happiness or misery in this life.

"For love, nor honor, wealth, nor power,
Can give the heart a cheerful hour
When health is lost. Be timely wise;
With health all taste of pleasure flies."

Moreover, the mind is affected by the condition of the body, and the morals by the state of the mind. As, therefore, cooking determines to a large degree the condition of the body, it must also affect to a considerable extent our moral and spiritual welfare. It is not too much to say, therefore, that there is religion in good cooking.

It has been truly said that "the cook fills an important place in the household. She is preparing food to be taken into the stomach, to form brain, bone, and muscle. The health of all the members of the family depends largely upon her skill and intelligence." As the lives of those on a steamship are in the hands of the helmsman, so the lives and the health of the members of the family are, to a great degree, in the hands of the one who prepares their meals.

Thousands are dying annually as the result of poor cooking. Food poorly prepared is not nutritious, and can not, therefore, make good blood.

Some may say they have no natural ability to cook; but any one having ordinary intelligence, with a little effort, care, and proper directions, can learn to cook well. And surely the health of the family ought to be of sufficient importance to inspire every mother with ambition to learn how to cook.

Mothers should also teach their daughters the mysteries of good cooking. They should show them that this is an essential part of their education,—more essential than the study of music, fancy work, the dead languages, or the sciences. The knowledge of these latter without the knowledge of how to care for the body and provide it with suitable nourishment, is of little worth. Meredith hit upon a great truth when he said:—

"We may live without music, poetry, and art;
We may live without conscience, and live without heart,
We may live without friends; we may live without books;
But civilized man can not live without cooks."

No young woman should contemplate marriage until she has first acquired a practical knowledge of simple cookery, for this is essential, whether she expects to do the cooking herself, or supervise the maid. Although bread is the staff of life, it is a sad fact that a large proportion of the daughters of the present generation do not know how to make a good loaf of bread. They have not been instructed in the useful art of cookery, so that when they have families of their own they can provide for their tables a well-cooked dinner, prepared with nicety, so that they would not blush to place it before their most esteemed friends.

There has never been an age so noted for dyspeptics as the present, and there was perhaps never before a time when there was a greater scarcity of good cooks.

"Though we boast of modern progress as aloft we proudly soar
Above untutored cannibals whose habits we deplore,
Yet in our daily papers any day you chance to look
You may find this advertisement: 'Wanted—A Girl to Cook.'"

Good cooking does not consist in the preparation of highly seasoned foods to pamper a perverted appetite, but in cooking with simplicity, variety, and skill natural foods in a palatable and wholesome manner. To assist in this direction is the object of this little work.

But no workman can work without materials and tools. The necessary materials for cooking are indicated in the recipes given in this book. Illustrations of many of the most necessary and useful cooking utensils will be found scattered throughout the work.

A very convenient and easily constructed wall rack, which may be placed over the kitchen work table, is shown in the following cut:

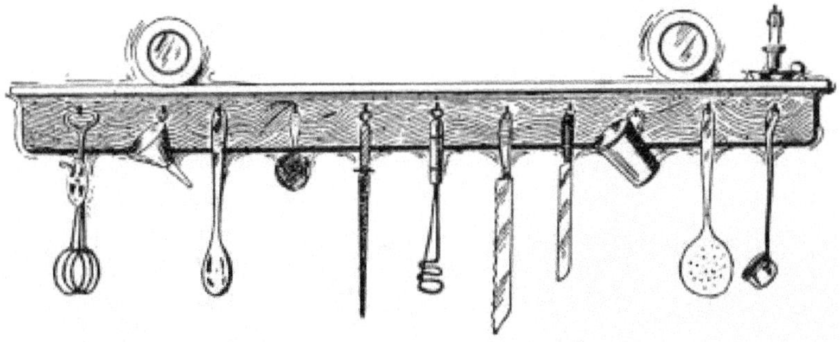

O hour of all hours, the most pleasant on earth,
Happy hour of our dinners!—*Meredith.*

Soup rejoices the stomach, and disposes it to receive and digest other food.—*BrillatSavarin.*

It is important that we relish the food we eat.—*ChristianT emperance.*

Soup is easily prepared, economical, and when made from healthful materials, is a very wholesome article of diet. It adds much to the elegance and relish of a dinner, and, if taken in small quantities, is a good means of preparing the whole system to assimilate a hearty meal.

Soups afford an excellent opportunity for using left-over foods which might otherwise be wasted. A combination of vegetables left over from the previous day, such as a cupful of mashed potatoes, some stewed peas, beans, or lentils, a few spoonfuls of boiled rice, stewed tomatoes, or other bits of vegetables or grains, if in good order, make a very palatable and nourishing soup. The vegetables should be put all together in a saucepan with enough water to cover them, let simmer for an hour or two, then rubbed through a colander, and returned to the saucepan with sufficient water added to make the soup of proper consistency, reheated, seasoned, and served.

For seasoning soup, a few spoonfuls of cream, or a little butter or nut butter may be used, though, if properly made, it is quite relishable without.

We wish all our readers success with the following simple but delicious kinds.

BEAN SOUP

For two quarts of soup soak one pint of beans overnight. In the morning drain, and put to cook in cold water, adding one-third cup of well-washed rice if desired; boil slowly for about two hours. When done, rub through a colander, thin with boiling water, and season with a little butter and salt.

POTATO SOUP

Pare and slice three medium-sized potatoes, and put to cook with a tablespoonful of chopped onion, or stalk of celery chopped fine, in sufficient water to cover. If celery is not at hand, one-half teaspoonful of celery salt may be used instead. Melt two tablespoonfuls of butter in a saucepan over the fire, then add two tablespoonfuls of flour, stir well, and cook one minute; then add gradually one quart of milk, stirring constantly until thickened. Simmer for ten minutes. As soon as the potatoes are done, and the water nearly absorbed, rub, without draining, through a colander, and add them to the hot, thickened milk. Season with salt, and serve.

GREEN PEA SOUP

Add to a quart of green peas a teaspoonful of sugar and enough water to cover; cook gently until tender, and the water quite absorbed. Then rub through a colander, add a quart of milk, salt to taste, and return to the fire. Heat to boiling, then add a spoonful of flour, mixed smooth with a little butter, then to a thin paste with a little of the soup. Simmer for a few minutes, and serve with croutons. If desired, a little onion or celery may be added for seasoning during the last few minutes of cooking, and then be removed.

SPLIT PEA SOUP

Wash one cupful of dried, split peas, and soak for several hours, or overnight, in cold water. Then put to cook in three pints of cold water, and boil slowly until thoroughly dissolved, adding more water occasionally to keep the quantity good. Stir up frequently from the bottom of the kettle. Rub through a colander; add water or rich milk to make the proper consistency, and return to the fire. Brown slightly one tablespoonful of flour in a tablespoonful of butter or cooking oil, then thin it with a few spoonfuls of the hot soup; stir this into the boiling soup, with salt to taste; simmer for ten minutes, and serve. An onion chopped fine and browned with the flour may be used for seasoning; also a cupful of tomatoes may be cooked with the peas before straining, if desired.

SPLIT PEA AND VERMICELLI SOUP

Make the soup as above. Cook one-half cup of vermicelli in a cupful of boiling water for ten minutes and add to the soup.

TOMATO SOUP

Put a quart can of tomatoes in a porcelain stewpan, add a pint of water, and stew until well done. Brown lightly in a frying-pan a tablespoonful of finely chopped onion in a tablespoonful of butter or cooking oil; then mix in a tablespoonful of flour or cornstarch; thin this with a little of the soup, and then stir it into the soup. Simmer for ten minutes, run through a colander, reheat, add salt to taste, and serve hot with croutons.

CREAM OF TOMATO SOUP

Take two cupfuls of canned or fresh tomatoes, add a cupful of water, one teaspoonful of minced onion, and, if desired, a little chopped celery; stew till tender, then rub through a colander. Heat one quart of milk to boiling. Have mixed smooth one tablespoonful of butter and one level tablespoonful of flour, then thin with a little of the hot milk. Stir this into the milk as soon as it starts to boil, and cook for several minutes, adding salt to taste. Then add the tomatoes. Do not cook or let stand after the tomatoes are added, but serve at once.

LENTIL SOUP

Cook one cupful of lentils, previously soaked an hour or two in about a quart of water, until tender. Rub through a colander; return to the fire, adding enough boiling water to make a quart in all, a small onion cut in slices, and salt to taste. When heated to boiling, thicken to the consistency of cream with browned flour. Season with a little butter or a few spoonfuls of sweet cream. If butter is used it should be mixed or braided with the flour, then thinned with enough of the soup so that it can be easily poured in. Simmer for ten minutes after adding the flour. Remove the onion before serving. The German or dark lentils are usually cheaper than the Egyptian or red lentils.

LENTIL AND TOMATO SOUP

Soak one cupful of lentils in cold water for a few hours, then cook in a quart of water until tender, with one small onion, three or four fresh tomatoes, or two cupfuls of stewed ones, and a tablespoonful of nut butter, if desired. Rub through a colander, add hot water to make three pints in all, reheat to boiling, and slightly thicken with a spoonful of browned flour mixed with a little cold water. Season with a small lump of butter or a few spoonfuls of cream.

TOMATO AND MACARONI SOUP

Drop a cupful of macaroni broken into small pieces into three or four cupfuls of boiling, slightly salted, water; boil from thirty to sixty minutes, or until tender, the length of time required depending upon whether the macaroni is fresh or stale. Have stewing one quart of fresh or canned tomatoes, and when done, rub through a colander; drain the macaroni, and add it to the tomatoes, with hot water to make about three pints in all. Reheat, season with salt and a little butter, and, after removing from the fire, add a few spoonfuls of sweet cream if convenient. Serve as soon as the cream is added.

RICE SOUP

Wash one-third cup of rice and put to cook in about three cupfuls of water, adding a little salt; cook until tender. Then add one quart of milk, and salt to taste; reheat to boiling. Have ready a tablespoonful of butter mixed smooth with a tablespoonful of flour, then made thin with a little of the hot milk; pour this into the soup and simmer for ten minutes. Celery may be added for flavoring if desired. Also, if desired richer, a beaten yolk of egg, first mixed with a few spoonfuls of the hot soup to prevent coagulating, may be added to the soup a few minutes before serving.

SAGO PEA SOUP

Wash, soak, and cook one cupful of split peas in plenty of water until tender; rub through a colander, return to the fire, adding enough hot water to make three pints in all, and a few slices of onion. Wash three tablespoonfuls of sago in warm water, and stir gradually into the soup; simmer for a half-hour, or until well dissolved. Remove the onion, and season with salt. Add a few spoonfuls of thin cream or rich milk to the beaten yolk of an egg, and stir into the soup a few minutes before serving.

SAGO FRUIT SOUP (SUMMER)

Soak one-half cup of sago for an hour in a cup of cold water; then add a quart of hot water, and simmer until transparent. In the meantime cook together one cup of prunes and one-half cup of raisins in a small quantity of water. When the sago is transparent, add the fruit, together with one-half cup of currant, plum, or some other tart fruit juice, and one-half cup of sugar. This will make three pints of soup. Serve hot with croutons.

Instead of the above, rice with dried apricots, and prune or currant juice may be used.

VEGETABLE SOUP (SUMMER)

Take a cupful each of chopped turnips, carrots, cauliflower or cabbage, several young onions cut fine, one cupful of green peas, one tablespoonful parsley or bay leaves for flavoring, and stew together in a stewpan with water to cover for six or eight minutes; then drain, cover with fresh boiling water, and stew slowly until tender, and the water nearly absorbed. Strain through a colander. Add enough hot rich milk or cream to make quite thin, salt to taste, reheat, and serve.

VEGETABLE SOUP (WINTER)

Put two tablespoonfuls of butter into a stewpan or soup kettle, add one onion chopped fine, and brown nicely; stir frequently to prevent burning. To this add a tablespoonful of flour, mix thoroughly, then pour in slowly a pint of hot water, stirring to keep smooth. Add to this one-half cupful each of chopped carrots, turnips, and celery, one cupful of tomatoes, a teaspoonful of salt, a tablespoonful of chopped or powdered parsley, bay leaves or thyme, and a slice of bread toasted very brown. Boil two potatoes for ten minutes, drain, and add them to the soup. Simmer all till well done, run through a colander, add hot water to make of proper consistency, a little more salt if desired, and serve hot.

VEGETABLE SOUP STOCK

Put into a kettle one quart of tomatoes, three pints of water, and place over the fire; add one onion, one or two pared potatoes, and one carrot, all finely chopped, one teaspoonful of celery salt, two bay leaves, and cook slowly for one hour. Run through a colander, and add salt to taste. Add to this cooked macaroni, spaghetti, vermicelli, corn, or rice.

BARLEY SOUP

Cook a cupful of pearl barley in three pints of water for several hours, adding water as needed to keep the quantity good. When done, add salt and a little cream, or the beaten yolk of an egg.

NOODLE SOUP

Beat the yolks of two eggs thoroughly, then add one cup of sifted flour, and knead well for five or ten minutes; divide into four parts, roll each part nearly as thin as a knife blade, and place on a clean cloth near the fire to dry. When dried sufficiently so that they will not stick together when rolled up, or be so dry as to be brittle, roll each piece up into a roll, and with a sharp knife cut or shave crosswise into very narrow slices, about one-twelfth of an inch in width. Shake out well, and let dry thoroughly. Then drop into hot salted water, and boil twenty minutes; drain off the water well, add a quart of milk, salt to taste, reheat, and serve. Noodles may be added to other soups instead of macaroni.

ASPARAGUS SOUP

Take two bundles of fresh, tender asparagus, wash, cut into short lengths, and put to cook in a quart of hot water. Let cook slowly till tender, and the water reduced one-half; rub through a colander, add three cups of milk, a spoonful or two of cream, and salt to taste. Let heat to boiling, and serve with croutons. A half cup of well-cooked rice may be stirred into the soup before serving if desired.

FOUNDATION FOR CREAM OF VEGETABLE SOUPS

Rub one tablespoonful each of butter and flour to a cream, then slowly pour into it one quart of boiling milk, stirring well. Allow to thicken, add salt to taste, and the seasoning and ingredients, as canned corn, peas, celery, asparagus, salsify, etc., desired for the soup. To make the soup richer, a beaten egg, or a few spoonfuls of cream may be put into the tureen before turning in the soup.

CROUTONS FOR SOUP

Cut bread into small cubes from one-half inch to an inch square, and brown in a moderate oven. A spoonful or two of the croutons may be placed in each plate, and the hot soup turned over them, or placed in a dish on the table for use as desired.

BROWNED FLOUR FOR SOUPS

Spread a small quantity of flour on shallow tins, and brown lightly in a moderately hot oven; stir often enough to prevent any part from scorching. A quantity may be prepared and put away in covered jars for use.

SEASONING FOR SOUPS

Ground nuts with herbs, dried and powdered nicely, flavor and enrich vegetable soups, gravies, and sauces.

HERBS FOR SOUPS

Herbs, such as bay leaves, parsley, thyme, etc., are valuable for flavoring soups, savories, and gravies. They can be obtained at a druggists, and a few cents' worth will last a long time.

"O stay me with rice and with porridge
O comfort me sweetly with grits!
Baked beans give me plenty of courage,
And cracked wheat enlivens my wits."

No one should adopt an impoverished diet.

Bring me my breakfast—oatmeal and boiled eggs.—*A. T. Stewart, the millionaire.*

Carlyle, catching a glimpse of Macaulay's face, once remarked, "Well, any one can see that you are an honest, good sort of a fellow, made out of oatmeal."

Dr. Johnson, who entertained a great dislike for the Scots, and lost no opportunity of saying bitter things against them, once defined oats as "in Scotland food for Scotchmen; but in England, food for horses." He was well answered by the indignant Scotchman, who replied, "Yes, and where can you find such men as in Scotland, or such horses as in England?"

Most grains require prolonged cooking, and slow cooking is preferable to fast. They are frequently served in the form of mush, and too often in an underdone state. Thorough cooking not only breaks up the food, but partially digests the starch contained in it.

Salt should be added to the water before stirring in the grain or meal.

All grains and meals should be put into actively boiling water to prevent them from having a raw taste, and allowed to boil fast until they "set," or thicken, and cease sinking to the bottom; till then they should be stirred frequently, but gently, to prevent burning. After the grain has thickened, it should be stirred very little, or none at all.

Enough grain or meal should be used to make the mush quite thick and glutinous when done. Watery or sloppy mush is neither palatable nor strengthening to the digestive organs when used constantly. In fact, it should not be considered necessary to have mush every morning. A change occasionally to drier foods is better for the digestion.

Double Boiler

An excellent utensil for cooking grains is a milk or mush boiler, generally called a double boiler. This consists of one vessel set inside of another, the inner one containing the grain to be cooked, the other partly filled with boiling water. An ordinary saucepan, however, will do very well, if smooth, and by greasing the inside with a little butter before putting in the water, the tendency of the grain to adhere to the saucepan will be greatly obviated.

If a double boiler is used, allow the grain to boil in the inner vessel standing directly over the range until it “sets,” then cover and place in the outer vessel, the water in which must also be boiling in order that the cooking process be not checked; then leave to cook slowly until done. From three to four hours is not too long when the double boiler is used. Grain prepared in this way may be cooked on the previous day and simply warmed up again the next morning for breakfast. What is left over from any meal may be used in the next preparation.

If a hastily prepared mush is required, perhaps nothing better than the rolled oats can be employed, these requiring not more than half an hour’s cooking, as they are already partially cooked in their manufacture; but even these are improved by longer cooking in a double boiler.

It is very important, when making any kind of mush, that the water be boiling rapidly, and kept thus while stirring in the meal; for unless the grain or meal is thoroughly scalded when stirred in, not even prolonged cooking will take away the raw taste.

OATMEAL MUSH

To a quart of boiling water add a pinch of salt, sprinkle in a cupful of oatmeal, and boil rapidly for about ten minutes, or until it sets, stirring frequently with a fork. Then place over the hot water in the lower boiler and cook from one to three hours. Just before serving, remove the cover and stir lightly with a fork to allow the steam to escape. This makes the mush more dry. Serve with baked apples, cream, fresh fruit, or with the juice from stewed fruit. Oatmeal is richer in nitrogen than any other grain, and therefore very nutritious. But to be wholesome it must be well cooked, and not served in a pasty, undone mass.

Quart Measure

ROLLED OATS

This is much preferred by some, as it requires only a short time to cook. Make as above, only using two cupfuls of the meal to one quart of water. An ordinary saucepan does very well for this, but the double boiler is better.

ROLLED OATS AND SAGO MUSH

Wash and soak one-third cup of sago in a little cold water. Stir one and one-half cups of rolled oats into one quart of salted, boiling water. Cook for fifteen minutes, then stir in the sago, and cook as much longer. Serve with cream, stewed fruit, or fruit juice.

GRAHAM MUSH

Into three pints of rapidly boiling water, properly salted, stir dry, one heaping pint of sifted Graham flour. Cook slowly for one hour on the back of the range, stirring but little after the first few minutes. Serve with milk or cream, and a very little sugar if desired.

GRAHAM MUSH WITH DATES

Cook as above. Take a cupful of dates, cut in two, removing the stones, and stir into the mush just before taking from the fire. Serve with milk or cream. Steamed raisins or stewed figs may be used instead of dates. Serve hot, or pour out into cups or molds, first wet with cold water, and serve cold with cream.

BOILED RICE

Wash one cup of rice, and put to cook in four cups of boiling water, slightly salted. Cook quite rapidly for the first fifteen minutes, stirring a little occasionally to prevent sticking to the pan. Then cover closely, and cook slowly on the back of the range without stirring. When nearly done, add a cup of sweet milk, cook until tender, and serve with milk, cream, or stewed fruit. If the rice has been soaked overnight, put to cook in an equal quantity of boiling water, or equal parts of milk and water, and cook for about half an hour.

CREAM OF WHEAT

To four parts of boiling water previously salted, add one part cream of wheat, sprinkling it in with the hand, and cook slowly for about an hour. Serve hot with cream or stewed figs.

CORN-MEAL MUSH, NO. 1

Into three pints of boiling water, salted, sprinkle one pint of corn-meal. Cook slowly for an hour, stirring occasionally. Serve with plenty of milk or cream. Very good and nutritious, especially for winter.

CORN-MEAL MUSH, NO. 2

Put to boil one quart of water, adding one teaspoonful of salt. Mix smooth one tablespoonful of flour and two cupfuls each of milk and corn-meal. Stir this gradually into the rapidly boiling water; boil about half an hour, stirring frequently. Serve as soon as done, with rich milk.

CORN-MEAL SQUARES

Take cold, left-over corn-meal mush, cut into rather thick slices, and then into inch squares. Put the squares into a tureen, and pour over them some hot milk or cream. Cover the dish, let stand a few minutes, and serve.

BARLEY MUSH

To each cupful of pearl barley, previously washed, add five cups of boiling water, a teaspoonful of salt, and cook in a double boiler for three or four hours. Serve with cream, lemon sauce, or stewed fruit.

BOILED WHEAT

To one part of good, plump wheat add five parts of cold water, a little salt, and cook slowly from four to six hours, or until the grains burst open and are tender. If soaked overnight, less time for boiling will be required. Add a little more water while cooking if necessary, but avoid much stirring. Serve hot or cold with milk, cream, fruit, or fruit juice. A very simple and wholesome dish.

GLUTEN MUSH

Into three pints of rapidly boiling, salted water stir one pint of gluten; cook in a double boiler for several hours.

HOMINY

Soak, then put to cook in enough boiling water to cover. Cook gently for several hours, being careful not to stir after the grains begin to soften. Add a little more water if needed. Season with salt when done. A quantity may be cooked at a time, and warmed up with a little cream or butter as needed.

CRACKED WHEAT

Cook the same as hominy and oatmeal, using three parts of boiling water to one of cracked wheat. When done, turn into cups or molds first wet with cold water. Nice served cold with cream. Seedless raisins may be cooked with it.

GRANULATED WHEAT

Use the same proportion and cook the same as cracked wheat. Serve warm or cold with good sweet cream.

CORN-MEAL CUTLETS

Cut cold corn-meal mush into slices three inches long and one inch wide; roll each piece in beaten egg, slightly salted, then in grated bread crumbs; place on an oiled tin in the oven till nicely browned. Other mushes may be treated likewise.

BROWNED RICE

Place a small quantity on shallow tins, and brown in the oven till a golden yellow, stirring frequently so that it may brown evenly; then steam for about an hour in a steamer over boiling water or in a steam cooker, allowing two parts of hot water to one part of rice. When done, it should be quite dry and mealy. It may be eaten dry, or served with brown or lentil sauce, or rich milk or cream.

BAKED MUSH

Cook any of the foregoing mushes as directed, and as soon as done, turn into a pan, crock, or a round tin can, first wet with cold water, or oiled, to prevent sticking. If brushed over the top with oil, a crust will not form. When cold, cut into slices from one half to three fourths of an inch thick, place on oiled tins, and bake till a nice brown. A quart of cooked mush will make about a dozen slices.

TOASTS

"A meal—what is it? Just enough of food
   To renovate and well refresh the frame,
So that with spirits lightened, and with strength renewed,
   We turn with willingness to work again."

The appetite is subject to education; therefore learn to love that which you know to be good and wholesome.

The most *expensive* food is spoiled when served up burnt or tasteless; the *cheapest* may be delicious with the proper seasoning.—*Lantz.*

Toast makes a very nice breakfast dish, and is easily and quickly prepared. It can be made in a variety of ways which are both simple and wholesome. When properly prepared, it furnishes abundant nourishment, and is easily digested.

The proper foundation for all toasts is zwieback (pronounced zwībäck), or twice-baked bread. This may be made from either fresh or stale bread, the fresh making the more crisp and delicious for dry eating. The bread should be light and of good quality. That which is sour, heavy, and unfit to eat untoasted, should never be used for toast.

Toasts afford an excellent opportunity for using up left-over slices of bread, and its use is therefore a matter of economy as well as of securing variety in diet.

ZWIEBACK, OR DRY TOAST

Cut fresh or stale light bread, either white or brown, into slices half an inch thick, place on tins, and bake slowly in a moderate oven until browned evenly throughout. Care should be taken not to scorch the bread. It should not be put into an oven that is merely warm. It should be baked, not simply dried. The common method of toasting merely the outside of the bread by holding it over a fire is not the most wholesome way of preparing toast. When properly made, it will be crisp throughout. Zwieback may be prepared in quantity and kept on hand for use. It furnishes a good article of diet, especially for dyspeptics, eaten dry, or with milk or cream.

MILK TOAST

Scald one cupful of milk in double boiler, then add one teaspoonful of cornstarch, mixed with a little cold water; stir until it thickens. Cook about ten minutes, then add one teaspoonful of butter, one-fourth teaspoonful of salt, and pour it over six slices of zwieback, previously moistened with hot water or milk.

TOAST WITH CREAM SAUCE

Prepare a cream sauce as directed on page 77. Moisten five or six slices of zwieback by dipping them quickly into hot water or milk, place them on a dish, and pour over the hot cream sauce.

ASPARAGUS TOAST

Prepare asparagus by washing each stalk free from sand; remove the tough portions, cut the stalks into small pieces, and stew in a little hot, salted water; drain off the water as soon as done, add a cup of milk, and season with a little butter and salt. Cream may be used instead of the milk and butter. Moisten the zwieback with hot milk, and place in a dish. Pour over the stewed asparagus, and serve hot.

BERRY TOAST

Prepare zwieback as above. Take fresh or canned strawberries, raspberries, mulberries, or other fruit, mash well with a spoon, add sugar to sweeten, and serve as a dressing on the slices of zwieback previously moistened.

EGG TOAST

Moisten slices of zwieback in hot milk or cream, season with a sprinkle of salt, and serve hot with a poached egg on each slice. For poached eggs see page 66.

BANANA TOAST

Moisten slices of zwieback in hot milk. Mash the bananas into a pulp, or cut into thin slices, and place some on each slice of toast.

FRUIT TOAST

Take stewed apricots, peaches, or plums, rub through a colander, heat to boiling, thicken with a little cornstarch, sweeten to taste, and pour over the moistened zwieback.

CREAM TOAST

Moisten slices of zwieback in hot water, sprinkle with a little salt, and dip over each slice a spoonful or two of nice, sweet, cold cream.

BUTTER TOAST

Place each slice of zwieback on a small plate, pour over a little hot water, and quickly drain off; add a sprinkle of salt, if desired, spread lightly with butter and serve.

CRUSHED TOAST

Take fresh, but thoroughly toasted bread or crackers, or some of each, grind closely in a coffee or hand mill, or crush with a rolling-pin, and serve in small dishes with milk, cream, or fruit juice. This may be served as a substitute for the health food known as granola. Crushed toast is also a very serviceable article for use in soups and puddings.

TOMATO TOAST

Moisten slices of zwieback in hot milk, and serve with a dressing prepared by heating a pint of strained, stewed tomatoes to boiling, and thickening with a tablespoonful of flour or cornstarch rubbed smooth in a little cold water. Season with salt and a little cream or butter, and pour over the toast.

BEAN PASTE

Soak one cupful of white beans overnight in cold water; put to cook in the morning in boiling water, and cook to a pulp, and till the water is quite absorbed. Rub through a colander, then add a tablespoonful of finely minced onion, one teaspoonful of powdered sage, one saltspoonful of celery salt, the juice of one lemon, two or three spoonfuls of tomato juice, if at hand, and salt to taste. Simmer together for a short time, then use cold to spread on toast or bread as a relish, or in the place of butter, or for making sandwiches.

VARIETY.—Remember, as Home Note says, that “variety of diet is important. Ill health often follows a monotonous sameness of diet. Oatmeal, bread and butter, and marmalade, are all excellent breakfast dishes of their kind, but when given every morning, for years at a time, they become positively nauseating.”

A VOICE FROM THE CORN

"I was made to be eaten, not to be drank,
To be thrashed in a barn, not soaked in a tank;
I come as a blessing when put in a mill,
As a blight and a curse when run through a still;
Make me up into loaves, and your children are fed;
But made into drink, I will starve them instead.
In bread I'm a servant, the eater shall rule,
In drink I'm a master, the drinker a fool.
Then remember my warning; my strength I'll employ,—
If eaten, to strengthen, if drunk, to destroy."

The wandering Arab lives almost entirely upon bread, with a few dates as a relish.

Behind the nutty loaf is the mill wheel; behind the mill is the wheat field; on the wheat field rests the sunlight; above the sun is God.—*James Russell Lowell.*

BREAD stands at the head of all foods. It has very properly been termed "the staff of life."

Why this is so is because wheat, from which bread is mostly made, contains more nearly than any other one article, all the necessary food elements required to sustain the human system, and these, too, in proper proportions, and so forms most nearly a perfect food. From it the brain, bones, muscles, and nerves, all receive a large amount of nourishment.

This being so, bread should enter largely into the daily bill of fare of every family. It is hardly too much to say that no meal is complete without it.

Where little bread is used, serious defects may frequently be observed. For instance, in some of the islands of the Pacific Ocean, where no wheat has been grown, and little could be obtained, the inhabitants almost universally have poor teeth. The early decay of the teeth so prevalent among the rising generation to-day, may generally be attributed to four causes: (1) A lack of sufficient lime in the water; (2) too free indulgence in sweets, such as rich cakes, jams, and candies; (3) too large an amount of flesh foods; and (4) an insufficient supply of good, simple, wholesome bread, especially whole wheat bread.

Home-made bread, when properly prepared, is generally to be preferred to bakers' bread. Chemicals and adulterations, as well as a lack of cleanliness and proper care in preparation, not infrequently characterize the latter, and thus give rise to serious stomach disorders. Moreover, bakers' bread is not always obtainable, and is always necessarily more expensive than that which is home-made. The baker can not afford to work for nothing. For these reasons, every woman, and especially every wife and mother, ought to know how to make good bread. The temptation to patronize the bake shop should not outweigh the interests of the health of the family, and the duty to practise economy.

The essentials to good bread-making are three:—

1. Good flour.
2. Good yeast.
3. Proper attention.

When either of these is lacking, good results can not be obtained. Poor flour will not produce good bread; good flour and poor yeast will not make good bread; and good flour and good yeast with improper attention will not insure good bread. All three are essential.

The first thing to consider in the making of bread is the flour. Good flour will generally be found to have a creamy white tint. That which is of a bluish white is seldom the best. Good flour will fall light and elastic from the hand. Flour that retains the imprint of the fingers when squeezed, and falls in a damp, clammy mass, should be avoided.

The second essential is good yeast. One may have ever so good flour and yet make poor bread, if the flour is used in conjunction with poor yeast. Good yeast has a fresh, pungent odor, and is light and foamy; while poor yeast has a sour odor, and a dull, watery appearance.

The third essential is proper attention. In winter, bread sponge should be made at night if it is desired to have the bread baked in the early part of the day. The flour used in making the sponge should first be warmed, and the sponge covered with several thicknesses of cloth, and set in a warm place till morning.

In hot weather set the sponge early in the morning, and the bread can be baked by noon. Both the sponge and dough are best kept in an earthen crock or jar, as they are less quickly affected by drafts of air.

As soon as the sponge has risen to be light and puffy, it should receive attention immediately, if desired to have the bread white and sweet. If allowed to reach the point of running over, or falling in the center, it has stood too long. For this reason sponge set at night should be mixed late in the evening, and attended to as early in the morning as possible.

In using very active yeast, it will not be necessary to set a sponge. Mix the ingredients into a good bread dough at the first mixing, beating the batter well while stirring in the flour. The more thoroughly the batter is beaten, the less kneading the dough will require. Set the bread in this way in the morning, and it can be baked by noon.

A few mealy potatoes, cooked and mashed, added to the sponge, makes the bread sweeter and keeps it fresh longer. Milk used in connection with yeast should first be scalded and cooled to lukewarm.

Too much flour should not be used in mixing, as it will make the bread hard and tough; but enough should be used to make the dough firm and elastic. Turn the dough out on the molding-board and knead it, not with the tips of the fingers, but with the whole hands, from the sides into the center, turning frequently, that all portions may be thoroughly worked. When the dough is smooth and elastic, with no dry flour left on its surface, form into a smooth ball, and place back in the crock, which should be washed clean, dried and oiled, to prevent the dough from sticking. Observe how full it makes the crock; cover up warmly, and when it has doubled its bulk, form gently into loaves, handling the dough as little as possible, and place in the pans for the last rising. When the loaves are risen to twice their size, place in a moderately hot oven to bake. The oven should be hot when the bread is put in. By no means have the bread, when ready to bake, wait for the oven to be heated, as it may then become too light, run over in the oven, and possibly be sour.

When nearly ready to bake, test the oven by putting in it a piece of writing-paper; if it turns dark brown in six minutes, the oven is of about the proper heat. If bread bakes too fast, a crust is formed on the outside of the loaf which prevents the inside from becoming hot enough to dry thoroughly, and the result is that the inside of the loaf is too moist, while the outside is baked hard. Bread should not brown much under fifteen or twenty minutes after being placed in the oven. If it rises much after being put in the oven, the heat is not sufficient. Bread should be turned around in the oven if it does not rise or brown evenly.

Medium-sized loaves should be baked from fifty to sixty minutes; small French loaves about thirty-five minutes. Bread is done when it shrinks from the pan, and can be handled without burning the fingers.

When taken from the oven, the loaves should be turned out of the pans, placed on their sides, so that the crust will not soften by the steam, and covered with a thin cloth. When cold, keep in a covered stone jar or a tin box, which should be kept free from crumbs and musty pieces of bread, and scalded and dried thoroughly every few days.

As to their healthfulness, the most wholesome breads are unleavened breads, or those made without either yeast, baking-powder, soda, or cream of tartar, such as gems, rolls, and crackers. Next come those made with good yeast; then those with baking-powder, if comparatively pure; and lastly those made with soda and sour milk, or soda and cream of tartar. Baking-powder is preferable to soda. The latter should seldom if ever be used, as it is injurious to the health, being an active dyspepsia-producing article.

WHITE BREAD

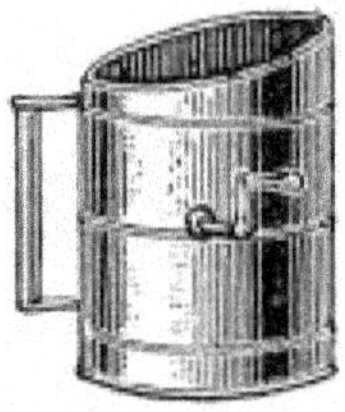

Flour Sieve

Scald a quart of new or unskimmed milk, let cool to lukewarm, then stir in a dissolved yeast cake, two teaspoonfuls of salt, and enough sifted flour to make a thin batter. Cover, and set aside till light, then work in flour until a dough of the proper consistency for bread is formed. Knead until it is smooth and elastic, and does not stick to the hands or board. Place in a clean, oiled crock, and when light, form into four loaves; let rise again and bake. Equal parts of milk and water may be used if desired.

MOTHER'S BREAD

In the evening boil three small potatoes, or save them out when cooking, and mash them with a fork in a gallon crock. Put in about three cupfuls of flour, two tablespoonfuls each of salt and sugar, then pour in enough boiling water to make a good batter. Beat until smooth. Soak one cake of compressed yeast or yeast foam in one-half cup of lukewarm water, and when the batter is just warm stir in the yeast and beat until quite foamy. Set in a warm place overnight. The first thing in the morning dip about two quarts of flour in a pan, make a cavity in the center, and pour in the sponge and about a pint of warm water. Stir all together into a thin batter, and set in a warm place till after breakfast; then knead until it does not stick to the board, put it in a three-gallon crock, well oiled to prevent the dough from sticking; cover with a tin lid to keep a crust from forming over the top, then with several thicknesses of cloth, and set in a warm place until it rises up full. Then mold into loaves, place in pans, let rise again, and bake in a moderate oven for about an hour, or until the loaves shrink from the sides of the pans and do not burn the fingers when removing from the pans. Turn the bread out of the pans, and cover with a thin cloth. This will make six loaves. If the loaves are brushed over with cold water just before being placed in the oven the crust will be more crisp.

GRAHAM BREAD, NO. 1

Take two tablespoonfuls of good liquid yeast, two cups of sweet milk, previously scalded and cooled to lukewarm, one teaspoonful of salt, and two cupfuls of white flour; beat together thoroughly, and set to rise. When very light, add three heaping cupfuls of sifted Graham flour, or sufficient to make a soft dough. Knead for a half-hour, then place in a pan slightly buttered, cover warmly, and set to rise. When light, form into loaves, let rise again, and bake.

GRAHAM BREAD, NO. 2

Make a sponge as for white bread. When light, add the stiffly beaten white of one egg, one tablespoonful each of sugar and melted butter, and enough sifted Graham flour to make a soft dough. Knead lightly, place back in oiled crock till light, then make into loaves, let rise, and bake. Graham bread should not be mixed as stiff as white bread, or it will be too solid. Two tablespoonfuls of molasses may be used for sweetening instead of sugar, if preferred.

GRAHAM FRUIT BREAD

Make the same as Graham bread, and when ready to form into loaves, add a cupful of raisins or dried currants, washed and dried, and dusted with flour.

WHOLE WHEAT BREAD

Make a sponge as for white bread. If desired a light color, use one fourth white flour instead of all whole wheat flour. Knead well, keeping the dough soft, then set in a warm place to rise. When light, form into loaves, let rise again, and bake. This bread rises slower than white bread.

BOSTON BROWN BREAD

Pint Measure

Scald one pint of corn-meal with a pint of boiling water; let cool till lukewarm, then stir in one dissolved yeast cake, or one-half cup of sweet, lively yeast, three tablespoonfuls of molasses, one teaspoonful of salt, and about three cupfuls of rye meal. Beat well, put in oiled pan, steam four or five hours, then place in the oven for half an hour to form a crust.

PARKER HOUSE ROLLS

Take two cupfuls of lukewarm milk, previously scalded, three tablespoonfuls of melted butter, or vegetable oil, one well-beaten egg, three tablespoonfuls of sugar, a pinch of salt, and one cake of yeast dissolved in a little of the milk; mix all together, then add enough flour to make a good batter. Let rise until light, knead, using sufficient flour; let rise again till very light, roll out to one-half inch in thickness, cut into round or oval shapes with a cutter, fold one third back over the top, and place in a pan to rise. When very light, bake in a moderate oven. Brush over with beaten yolk of egg, mixed with two spoonfuls of cold water just before taking from the oven. Braided or plaited rolls may be made by cutting the rolled dough into strips six inches long and one inch wide, pinching the ends of each three strips together, and then braiding.

CORN-MEAL BREAD

Stir one-half cup of corn-meal into two cupfuls of boiling water; when well cooked, remove from the fire and add two cupfuls of cold water; stir well together; then add one teaspoonful of salt, one cake of yeast dissolved in a little warm water, two tablespoonfuls of sugar or molasses, and enough white flour to make a good dough. Knead well, and set to rise; when light, form into three loaves, let rise again, and bake for nearly an hour.

SALT-RISING BREAD

Take a small pitcher and put into it a half pint of warm water, a teaspoonful each of salt and sugar, then stir in flour enough to make a medium-thick batter. Set the pitcher in a kettle of warm water to rise. It should be kept warm all the time, not hot, for if it is scalded, it will never rise. When light, stir in a pint of warm milk or water and enough warm flour to make a soft dough. Knead it, form into a loaf, place in the pan, set to rise in a warm place, and bake as soon as light.

RAISED BISCUITS

Make from dough prepared for white bread. When the dough is ready to form into loaves, divide it into small, equal portions, shape into smooth, round biscuits, place closely in a shallow baking pan, and let rise till considerably lighter than bread; brush lightly with milk, and bake in a rather quick oven.

GEMS
General Directions

Beating in an abundance of cold air is very essential in the making of good gems, as it is this that makes them light. Cold air is preferable to warm air, as it expands more when heating.

Gems are also better when baked in iron pans than in tin, as the iron retains the heat better, and bakes the gems more evenly. The irons should be heated and oiled before the batter is dropped into them.

Gem Irons

Having the oven hot from the first is also essential, as a crust will then be formed immediately, and the air which has been beaten into the batter will thus be prevented from escaping. They should be placed in the oven so as to bake on the top first, and afterward on the bottom. These points should be carefully observed. Gems are best served hot. They should be broken open, and never cut with a knife, as this makes them heavy.

GRAHAM GEMS, NO. 1

Place the gem irons in the oven or on the range to heat. Mix salted Graham flour with cold milk or water to a batter thick enough to drop, beating vigorously for ten minutes to beat in the air. Butter the gem irons, and fill each cup nearly full of the batter. Put in a hot oven, and bake until done.

GRAHAM GEMS, NO. 2

Beat separately the yolk and white of an egg. Add to the beaten yolk two cupfuls of sweet, rich milk, one-half teaspoonful of salt, and stir well together; then sift in one and one-half cups of Graham flour, and a scant cup of white flour, beating vigorously meanwhile. Continue to beat until the mixture is light and foamy throughout, and full of air bubbles; then stir in gently the stiffly beaten white of the egg. Have the gem irons thoroughly heated, slightly butter them, drop in the batter with a spoon, and bake in a quick oven.

OATMEAL GEMS

Beat separately the yolk and white of an egg. To the beaten yolk add a cupful of well-cooked oatmeal mush, and a half cup of milk or thin cream. Beat together thoroughly. Continue to beat while adding a cupful of white flour and a pinch of salt, then fold in lightly the stiffly beaten white of the egg. Have the gem irons heated hot, slightly butter, drop in the batter, filling the little cups nearly full, and bake in a quick oven until a light brown.

CORN-MEAL GEMS

Stir well together one and one-half cupfuls of milk, and the yolks of two eggs previously beaten. To this add two cupfuls of corn-meal, one-half teaspoonful of salt, and one cupful of white flour. Beat thoroughly, then stir in lightly the whites of the eggs previously beaten to a stiff froth, and bake as above.

GRANULATED WHEAT GEMS

Mix together one cupful each of cold water and milk, and one-half teaspoonful of salt. Then add gradually two and one-half cupfuls of fine granulated wheat, beating continuously. Beat vigorously for ten minutes, then drop by spoonfuls into thoroughly heated, buttered gem irons, beating the batter briskly several times while dipping it in. Bake at once in a very hot oven.

RICE CAKES

Moisten one cup of well-cooked rice with two tablespoonfuls of cream or rich milk; add one tablespoonful of sugar, and mix in enough flour to make it hold together. Form into cakes one-third of an inch thick, and bake in a hot oven. When done, split open, and serve with maple or lemon sirup. To make lemon sirup, see page 40.

BREAKFAST ROLLS

To three slightly heaping cups of sifted Graham flour add a little salt, and one cup of milk or thin cream; cream is better. Stir the milk or cream into the flour, mixing it well with the flour as fast as poured in. Knead thoroughly, then divide the dough into three portions, and with the hands roll each portion over and over on the molding-board until a long roll from an inch to an inch and a half in thickness is formed. Cut into two- or three-inch lengths, and bake at once in a hot oven, in a baking pan dusted with flour, or better, on a perforated piece of sheet-iron made for the purpose, placing the rolls a little distance apart. Bake until a light brown. When done, do not place one on top of another.

Flour kneaded into cold Graham flour, oatmeal, or corn-meal mush makes very good breakfast rolls.

STICKS

Make the same as breakfast rolls, only rolling the dough to about the size of the little finger, and cutting into three- or four-inch lengths.

FRENCH ROLLS

Make a sponge at night of one-half cake of dry or one-half cup of good liquid yeast, the beaten white of one egg, two tablespoonfuls of melted butter, two tablespoonfuls of sugar, a little salt, and three cups of warm milk or water, and flour sufficient to make a soft dough. In the morning knead well and let rise again. When light, roll out the dough to about three fourths of an inch in thickness; cut into about four-inch squares with a sharp knife, butter the edges, and roll each corner up and over to the center; place on buttered tins, allow the rolls to become very light, and bake in a moderately hot oven. The sponge for this can be set in the morning if the yeast is very quick.

TO GLAZE ROLLS

When ready to bake, brush the rolls or biscuit lightly with milk; or, when nearly baked, brush with the yolk of an egg to which has been added two spoonfuls of cold water and half a teaspoonful of sugar. Return to oven till done.

MARYLAND OR BEATEN BISCUIT

Mix five cupfuls of white flour, one-half cupful of vegetable oil or butter, and one teaspoonful of salt to a very stiff dough with one cupful of cold water. Knead for twenty minutes, using no more flour for the molding-board; then beat hard with a wooden mallet or hammer for twenty minutes longer, until the dough is flat and of even thickness throughout; sprinkle over a little flour, fold half of the dough back evenly over the other half, and beat quickly around the edges, to keep in the air. Continue beating until the dough is brittle, and will snap if a piece is broken off quickly. Pinch off into pieces the size of a small walnut, work smooth, flatten on top with the thumb, prick with a fork, place on perforated tins a little distance apart, and bake in a moderate oven for nearly an hour, or until dry and brittle throughout.

WHOLE WHEAT CRISPS

Take one cupful of rich cream, two tablespoonfuls of sugar, a pinch of salt, two cupfuls, or enough to make a stiff dough, of fine granulated, whole wheat flour. Beat well, and knead for fifteen minutes, first with a spoon, until the batter becomes too thick, and then with the hands. Roll out as thin as wafers, cut into shapes with a biscuit cutter, and bake on floured tins in a very hot oven.

GRAHAM WAFERS

Cake Cutter

Stir together one cupful each of sifted Graham flour and white flour, one tablespoonful each of butter and sugar, and a saltspoonful of salt; then mix with enough cold water to make a stiff dough. Roll out very thin, cut into small squares, or with a cake cutter, and bake on tins in a quick oven.

FRUIT BISCUIT

Make a dough with one cupful of cold, sweet cream or rich milk, three cupfuls of sifted Graham or white flour, and a little salt. Knead thoroughly, and divide into two portions. Roll each quite thin, then spread one with currants, stoned dates, figs, or seedless raisins, chopped fine, and place the other one on top; press down with the rolling-pin, cut into oblong squares with a knife, and bake.

CRESCENTS

Make a dough, using the recipe for White Bread. When ready to form into loaves, work into it two tablespoonfuls each of butter and sugar; roll out into a sheet half an inch thick, cut into six-inch squares, then divide diagonally, forming triangles; brush each lightly with water, and roll up, beginning at the longest side; place on oiled pans, turning the ends toward each other in the form of a crescent. When very light, brush with milk, and bake in a quick oven for about twenty minutes.

RUSKS

Make a sponge at night with one cupful of sugar, one cupful of scalded milk, cooled to lukewarm, one-half cupful of butter, two eggs, one cake of dry or one-half cup of good liquid yeast, and sufficient flour to make a drop batter. Set in a warm place to rise. In the morning knead well, and when risen again, mold into the form of biscuits, place a little distance apart on buttered tins, and brush over with the beaten white of an egg sweetened; let stand until light, and bake.

PLAIN BUNS

Beat together one-fourth cup of lively yeast, one cup of sweet milk, previously scalded and cooled to lukewarm, one-half teaspoonful of salt, two cups of warm flour, and set in a warm place to rise. When very light, work into the dough one-half cup of sugar, and two tablespoonfuls of butter. Knead well for ten minutes, using enough flour to make a soft dough. Shape into the form of biscuits a little larger than an egg; place on tins slightly buttered, and set in a warm place to rise. When very light, bake in a moderately hot oven. The tops may be brushed over with the sweetened beaten white of an egg while baking, or sprinkled with moist sugar when taken from the oven.

FRUIT BUNS

Make the same as plain buns, adding one-half cup of raisins or currants just before kneading and forming into buns.

RICE WAFFLES

Waffle Iron

Set a sponge at night with two cupfuls of sweet milk, scalded and cooled to lukewarm, one tablespoonful of butter, a pinch of salt, two-thirds of a cupful of boiled rice, three cupfuls of flour, and one-fourth cup of liquid yeast. Beat the batter hard for five or six minutes, and set in a warm place to rise. In the morning add two well-beaten eggs, and stir well together. Bake on a hot, buttered waffle iron. If this is not at hand, have the gem irons well heated, slightly butter to prevent sticking, and drop in the batter. Place in a hot oven so the top will bake first, and bake to a rich brown color. Very nice for breakfast.

PUFFS

To two cups of milk add a little salt and the yolks of two eggs well beaten; then sift in, a little at a time, and beating meanwhile, three small cups of flour. Beat until light, then stir in gently the stiffly beaten whites of the eggs, and bake in hot gem irons.

FRUIT LOAF, NO. 1

Take enough good bread dough for one loaf, add one cupful of brown sugar, two tablespoonfuls of butter, and one cupful of raisins, previously washed and dried. Knead well and let rise; then knead again, and place in a bread pan, let rise until light, and bake in a moderate oven.

FRUIT LOAF, NO. 2

Make a sponge of one and one-half cups of warm milk or water, one-half cup of good yeast, the beaten white of one egg, one tablespoonful each of butter and sugar, a little salt, and flour sufficient to make a soft dough. Let rise till light; then knead well and let rise again. When light, roll out to about one inch in thickness, spread over with chopped dates, or raisins, or currants which have been previously washed and dried; roll up and form into a loaf, let rise, and bake.

COFFEE CAKES

Take two cupfuls of bread dough (made with milk) when ready for the pans; put into a deep dish and work in four tablespoonfuls of cocoanut or vegetable oil or butter, four tablespoonfuls of sugar, the stiffly beaten white of one egg, and enough flour to make a fairly stiff dough. Knead well, and roll out into a long strip about nine inches in width, three feet in length, and one fourth of an inch thick; spread over this four or five tablespoonfuls of oil or melted butter, omitting about two inches at the farther end; beginning at end nearest, roll up like jelly roll; cut into slices an inch thick; place a little distance apart on tins sprinkled with sugar; set in a warm place, and when very light, brush over with oil; sprinkle with a little sugar, and bake. If desired, ground cinnamon or grated nutmeg may be sprinkled over the dough before rolling it up.

FLANNEL CAKES

Heat three cupfuls of milk to boiling; put into a crock one cupful of corn-meal and two tablespoonfuls of butter, then pour in the scalding milk; beat well, allow to cool to lukewarm, then stir in one tablespoonful of sugar, two of flour, one teaspoonful of salt, and one-half yeast cake dissolved in one-third cup warm water; beat well, and set to rise overnight. Bake on a hot griddle.

CORN-MEAL BATTER CAKES

Griddle

To two cups of cold corn-meal mush, add one cup of sifted flour, and a pinch of salt; beat well the yolks of two eggs, to which add two-thirds cup of milk, and stir into the mush; beat thoroughly until light and smooth, adding a little more milk if necessary, to make the batter of proper consistency. Then gently stir in the whites of the eggs beaten to a stiff froth, and bake in small cakes on both sides on a griddle, slightly buttered, or better still on a soapstone griddle, in which case use no oil nor butter on it. Serve hot.

BUCKWHEAT PANCAKES

In the evening take two quarts of warm water, add one-fourth cup of good yeast, a teaspoonful of salt, and buckwheat flour enough to make a good batter. If desired, a cupful of corn-meal or a few spoonfuls of white flour may be used instead of all buckwheat. Beat well and set to rise. In the morning thin the batter with a little warm water, if necessary, and bake on a hot griddle. If cakes are desired for several mornings, the batter may be kept going by leaving at least a cupful after each baking, and adding the necessary warm water and buckwheat flour each evening as at first.

LENTIL FRITTERS

To a pint of lentil soup (left-over soup will do), add the well-beaten yolks of two eggs, and sift in enough flour, a little at a time, beating thoroughly, to make a good batter. Then add the stiffly beaten whites of the eggs, drop by spoonfuls on a hot buttered griddle, and brown on both sides.

CORN FRITTERS

To each quart of raw sweet corn (a dozen nice ears), grated from the cob, add the beaten yolks of three eggs, a teaspoonful of salt, and one and one-half cups of fine bread or cracker crumbs, or enough to make a batter just stiff enough to drop from a spoon. Then stir in the stiffly beaten whites of the eggs, and drop with a spoon on a hot, oiled, or soapstone griddle. Serve hot.

USES FOR STALE BREAD

Whole slices of stale bread, if in good condition, may be steamed or used for toast. Crumbs, crusts, and broken pieces not suitable for this purpose may be placed in a pan, and put into a slow oven until thoroughly dried (not browned), then ground in a mill, or rolled on a breadboard with the rolling-pin, and put away in covered jars for use. This will be useful for making corn-meal cutlets or anything that is to be rolled in crumbs, dipped in egg, and browned.

POTATO YEAST

Put to cook six medium-sized potatoes in two quarts of hot water. Tie a handful of hops in a cloth, and boil with the potatoes during the last ten minutes. When done, take potatoes and hops from the water, leaving the water over the fire. Mash the potatoes fine, and add four tablespoonfuls of flour, and two each of sugar and salt. Stir well together. Pour over this mixture the boiling potato water, stirring well that no lumps be formed. When cooled to lukewarm, stir in a cupful of liquid yeast, or one cake of dry yeast dissolved in warm water. After fermentation has ceased, turn into an earthen jar previously scalded, cover, and set in a cool, dark place. Shake before using.

HOP YEAST

Steep a handful of hops in a quart of hot water for five minutes. Then strain, and turn the boiling water over a cupful of flour, blended with a little cold water. Add one tablespoonful of salt, and two of sugar; let cool till lukewarm, then stir in a half cup of liquid yeast, or one cake of dry or compressed yeast dissolved in a little warm water. Set aside for twenty-four hours, stirring occasionally; then bottle and keep as above.

FRUITS

The earth to thee her increase yields,
The trees their fruitage bring;
And glittering in the sunlit fields,
The vines with bounty spring.

"Every tree, in the which is the fruit of a tree yielding seed; to you it shall be for meat." Gen. 1:29.

If families could be induced to substitute the apple—sound, ripe, and luscious—for pies, cakes, candies, and other sweetmeats with which children are too often stuffed, there would be a diminution of doctor's bills, sufficient in a single year to lay in a stock of this delicious fruit for a season's use.—*Professor Faraday.*

There is much false economy; those who are too poor to have seasonable fruits and vegetables, will yet have pie and pickles all the year. They can not afford oranges, yet can afford tea and coffee daily.—*Health Calendar.*

FRUITS are a natural food. They form no inconsiderable part of those products of the earth given by the Creator to our first parents as food. "Behold, I have given you," he says, "every herb bearing seed, which is upon the face of all the earth, and every tree, in the which is the fruit of a tree yielding seed; to you it shall be for meat." Gen. 1:29.

Fruits are not only delightful to the eye, pleasing to the smell, and satisfying to the taste, but they contain elements which are necessary for the best maintenance of the system; hence the natural craving for them when the system is in a normal condition.

While not containing a large amount of nutrition compared to their size, they are, nevertheless, valuable on account of their juices, and also because of their giving bulk to our food,—a very necessary thing to be considered.

Containing as they do from seventy-five to ninety per cent of water, their use naturally allays thirst. If their use were more general, there would doubtless be less desire for unnatural drinks.

As a rule fruits, especially acid and sub-acid fruits, are cooling to the blood, and most kinds also act as a laxative to the system, tending to keep it free and open. They should, therefore, be freely used in the daily bill of fare, though in proper combinations. Fruits go well with grains and milk, but not so well with vegetables, especially acid fruits.

And what gives a nicer appearance to the table than a dish of fruit! The very sight is inviting and appetizing.

Fruit Dish

In preparing fresh fruit for the table, care should be taken to select only that which is sound and ripe. It should also be carefully cleaned. Apples should be wiped with a damp cloth, and their beauty will be further enhanced by polishing them with a dry one. Plums should be likewise treated. Grapes should be washed, and the stem ends of bananas cut off. Bananas may also be peeled, sliced, and served with cream. Oranges may be placed on the table whole, or their skins cut into eighths, and peeled half-way down. In serving cherries in their natural state, the stems should be left on.

Much taste may be displayed in the arrangement of fresh fruits for the table. A few green leaves interspersed with the fruit, or a variety of fruits tastily arranged on the same dish, make a very attractive appearance.

Nature sets before us an abundance of delicious fruits, and these in almost endless varieties and flavors.

Most fruits are both wholesome and agreeable when eaten raw, but many are rendered more easy of digestion by cooking. Some persons with weak digestion can not eat many kinds of raw fruits, but almost every one can eat most kinds when cooked.

The following are some of the most simple and practical ways in which fruits may be prepared:—

BAKED APPLES, NO. 1

Apples to be baked may be cored and pared or baked with the skins on. If firm and quite tart, pare, place in a pie dish, add sugar and a little hot water, and bake in a moderate oven. If the apples are juicy, less water will be required. When tender, turn into a dish, and pour over them the sirup or juice.

BAKED APPLES, NO. 2

Pare and core without halving, a number of nice, tart apples; fill the centers with sugar and jelly, lay closely in a shallow pan, add a little water, and bake slowly, basting occasionally with the sirup to keep the centers well filled. Bake till brown and tender, and serve with a boiled custard made with two cups of milk, two tablespoonfuls of sugar, two eggs, and vanilla to flavor.

STEWED APPLES

Pare, core, and cut into small pieces some moderately tart apples, place in a saucepan, and add sufficient boiling water to stew to a pulp; cook slowly for about an hour, stirring but little. When cool, add sugar to sweeten.

BAKED SWEET APPLES

Select good, sweet apples. Wash, but do not pare or core them; put into a baking pan with a little water, and bake in a hot oven. Baste occasionally with the juice in the bottom of the pan. When done, if desired, each apple may be dipped in the beaten white of an egg, then in powdered sugar, and returned to the oven until the icing is set. Plain sweet baked apples are very nice served with cream.

APPLE SCALLOP

Pare, core, and slice a half dozen good cooking apples. Spread a layer in the bottom of a deep pudding dish, then over these a layer of bread crumbs mixed with a little sugar, thus alternating till the dish is filled, having a layer of apples on top. Add a half cup of cold water, and bake in a rather quick oven till done. Serve with rich milk or cream.

BOILED APPLES

Remove the cores and cook whole, or in halves, in enough boiling water to cover them. Cook slowly. When tender, remove the apples to a dish with a spoon or fork. Sweeten the juice with sugar, add a little lemon extract, thicken slightly with a very little cornstarch blended with a little cold water, and pour over the apples. Serve when cool.

BAKED PEARS

Take good, sound pears, cut in halves, pare, and fill an enameled pudding dish, sprinkling sugar through them; pour in a cupful of hot water, cover tightly, and bake slowly till tender. Serve cold. Or wash, wipe, and bake whole in a shallow dish, putting in a very little water.

STEWED PEARS

Pare, quarter, and core nice ripe pears, and drop into cold water to keep from discoloring. Make a sirup, allowing two cups of water and a half cup of sugar to each quart of fruit. Boil the sirup for a few minutes, put in the fruit, and cook until tender and pink in color, being careful not to break the fruit by stirring. Three or four slices of lemon added to the sirup while boiling will improve the flavor of the pears. Remove the lemon before putting in the fruit.

BAKED QUINCES

Pare, core, and bake the same as apples. The fruit may be left whole, and the centers filled with sugar. Sufficient water should be used so the fruit will not become dry. Baste with the sirup while baking.

BAKED PEACHES, NO. 1

Take good, firm peaches, pare, cut in halves, removing the stones, and place in a deep pudding dish, sprinkling with sugar. Add a little water, and bake until tender.

BAKED PEACHES, NO. 2

Bake as above; when done, cover the top with a meringue made of the whites of two or three eggs beaten stiff and a little powdered sugar; return to the oven and brown slightly. Serve cold with cream.

STEWED PEACHES

Take ripe peaches, pare, or wipe carefully with a damp cloth; cut in halves, remove the stones, and drop into cold water. When ready, place the fruit in a saucepan, adding sufficient boiling water to keep from burning. Add sugar, two tablespoonfuls to each quart of fruit. Cook slowly until tender, generally from twenty to thirty minutes.

STEWED PRUNES

Wash the prunes thoroughly in warm water, rinse, then add water to cover, or about three parts water to one of prunes, and soak for several hours, or overnight. Put them to cook in the same water in which they soaked, and stew gently until tender. When nearly done, add a little sugar if desired. Serve cold.

STEWED FRUITS

Small fruits are better stewed in a double enamel saucepan, and the larger kind baked in a tightly covered earthen crock or jar in the oven, with as little water as possible. Dried fruit, such as figs, prunes, peaches, raisins, dates, etc., should first be well washed, rinsed, soaked for several hours in enough water to cover, and afterward cooked in the same water in which they have soaked.

PINEAPPLE

Pare, cut into thin slices into a dish, and sprinkle lightly with sugar; let stand in a cool place for an hour, and serve.

FRUIT MOLD

Stew a quart of berries in a small quantity of water for fifteen or twenty minutes; then add sugar to taste, and two tablespoonfuls of cornstarch dissolved in a little cold water; cook until thickened, then turn into molds first wet with cold water; serve cold with milk or cream. Heat fruit juices and treat similarly.

BANANAS WITH WHIPPED CREAM

Remove the peel, cut into thin slices, and sprinkle with a very little sugar and a few drops of orange juice. Serve in small dishes, placing a tablespoonful of whipped cream on each dish. If bananas are slightly scraped after removing the skins, they will be more readily digested.

APPLE BUTTER

Large Spoon

Pare, quarter, and core about equal parts of sweet and tart apples. Boil sweet cider down, about four gallons into one gallon. Cook the apples in either sweet cider or water till soft, then add the boiled cider, and boil and stir with a wooden spoon until thick. A little butter and ground cinnamon may be added for flavoring, and sugar if necessary. Can in jars, or set away in jars without canning if desired for immediate use.

LEMON SIRUP

Boil one cupful of sugar and one-fourth cupful of water until it slightly thickens; add a small teaspoonful of butter and a tablespoonful of lemon-juice. Serve hot.

LEMON HONEY

Put two tablespoonfuls of butter into a saucepan to warm; then add one cup of sugar, the juice and grated rind of two lemons, and two eggs well beaten; cook until thickened, stirring constantly that no lumps be formed, and, if not cooked in a double boiler, being careful not to burn. When done, turn into cups and cover the same as jelly. Nice used as a filling for layer cake.

PLUM MARMALADE

Wash the plums, cut them in halves, removing the stones, and cook for about fifteen minutes, allowing a scant cup of water to each quart of fruit. Then rub through a colander, add one cup of sugar to each quart of pulp, and boil slowly one hour, stirring often to prevent burning.

GRAPE MARMALADE

Make the same as plum marmalade, only allowing half a cup of water to a quart of fruit for cooking.

TO MAKE FRUIT JELLY

Choose a bright, sunny day for making jelly, in order to have it as firm and clear as possible. Make in small quantities at a time, using only porcelain or graniteware in preparing fruit or juice. Small fruits should be used as soon after being picked as possible, and should not be overripe. Cherries should be mixed with one fourth their quantity of currants, as they do not jelly easily. Two parts red raspberry with one part currant juice makes a nice-flavored jelly. Place the fruit desired for the jelly in the saucepan, add only enough water to keep from burning, and cook until tender or well scalded; then drain through a strong, coarse, white flannel or cotton bag first wrung out of hot water. If the bag is made three-cornered, the weight of the fruit at the large top presses the juice out more freely at the point. Heat the sugar in the oven, stirring frequently to prevent burning. About three fourths of a pound should be used to each pint of juice. To prevent the jelly glasses from breaking, place them in a pan of cold water and allow it to come nearly to boiling; or with a cloth rub the outside of them well with a little butter or oil, and pour in the juice slowly. A little paraffin poured over the jelly when cooled, or writing-paper cut to fit the glasses, and oiled, is good for covering before putting on the covers.

APPLE JELLY

Select nice tart, red apples, wash, quarter, and core, but do not pare; add a small quantity of water, and boil only until soft. Then strain as directed for making fruit jelly, measure the juice, return it to a clean saucepan, and boil for ten or fifteen minutes, skimming thoroughly. Add the heated sugar, three-fourths pound to each pint of juice. Boil a few minutes, or until it jellies nicely, then turn into glasses.

CURRANT JELLY

Weigh the fruit, and to each pound weigh out half the weight of granulated sugar. Place a few of the currants in a granite saucepan, mash with a potato masher to extract enough juice to keep it from burning, then add the remainder of the fruit, and boil about twenty minutes, stirring frequently to prevent burning; strain, return juice to a clean saucepan, let boil for five minutes, skim, then add the sugar previously heated. This should jelly at once. Turn into glasses. Make blackberry and raspberry jelly in the same way.

QUINCE JELLY

Wash, wipe, and remove any imperfect spots, quarter and core, but do not pare the fruit. Cut into small pieces, and place in the preserving pan, with water enough to half cover. Cook until tender, stirring frequently. Remove from the fire, and strain through a jelly-bag, measure the juice, return to a clean saucepan, let boil fifteen minutes, then add sugar, three-fourths pound to each pint of juice. Boil until it jellies nicely, removing the scum, and when done, turn into the jelly cups at once.

CRANBERRY JELLY

Pick over and wash one quart of cranberries, and put them in a granite saucepan with one cupful of boiling water; cook about ten minutes, or until soft. Then put them through a strainer or vegetable press, return the juice to the pan, add two cupfuls of sugar, place over the fire, and cook about five minutes. Turn into a mold to cool.

HOW TO CAN FRUIT
General Remarks

Boiling or canning fruit consists in sealing up in air-tight bottles, or jars, fruit which has previously been cooked. Many do not appreciate the value of canning fruit because they have never tried it. But the process is so simple, and the result so satisfactory, that those who have ever given it a trial usually feel well repaid for the effort put forth.

Canning fruit practically lengthens the fruit season until it is perennial. Fruit, if properly canned, can be preserved, even for years, in a very natural and wholesome state.

While it is true that in semitropical countries some kind of fruit can be obtained from the markets at most seasons of the year, it is both a matter of providence and economy to lay by, at a time when fruit is cheap and in season, for those times when it is scarce, high-priced, or unobtainable. A lesson can here be learned from the bee. During the summer, when the flowers are in bloom, it culls the sweet, that it may have a store of honey to eat in the winter hours.

It is very desirable to have the fruit fresh, as picked from the tree or vine; but many of the nicest and most juicy and delicately flavored fruits, such as strawberries, raspberries, currants, gooseberries, plums, blueberries, cherries, peaches, and apricots are in season for only a comparatively short time. It is, therefore, of value to know how to preserve these for the unseasonable portions of the year. It is a matter of no little convenience for the housewife to have these delicious fruits in her house, ready for use at a moment's notice. But this can be the case only by having on hand a supply of canned fruit.

Some may think that this supply of canned fruit can readily be substituted by the same kinds of fruit put up in jams, marmalades, etc., and that these can be purchased at reasonable prices at the stores all ready for use, and the trouble of preserving fruit one's self is thereby saved. While this may be true, the fruit prepared thus is not to be compared to fruit in its more natural state. The amount of sugar generally used in making jams and marmalades causes them to be too rich in saccharine matter, and consequently more liable, if freely used, to injure the teeth, cause acidity of the stomach, dyspepsia, and liver trouble, while nearly all, even dyspeptics, can eat simple stewed fruit of one kind or another without injury.

Selecting Cans

In canning fruit, care should be taken to provide good cans and perfectly fitting covers. This is a matter of much importance. The Mason glass cans, or jars, with the white porcelain-lined covers and white rubber bands, are, perhaps, the best. It may seem a little expensive on the start to purchase these, but there is practically no further expense connected with them, aside from providing new rubbers or covers occasionally, as the jars can be used year after year, or until broken. Either the pint, quart, or two-quart jars may be used, as best suits the needs of the family.

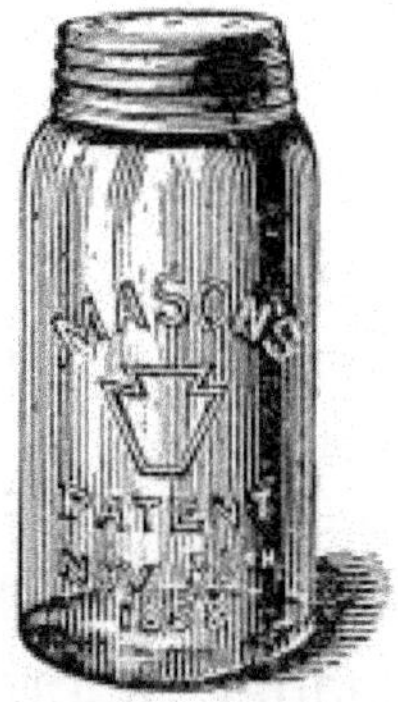

Mason Can

If a Mason can opener is not at hand, the process of opening the jars may be made easier by first running the edge of a thin knife blade around under the rubbers, care being taken not, by prying or otherwise, to injure the rubbers or lids.

After the fruit has been used from the jars, wash and dry them, and set away for future use. The rubbers and covers may be put into a cloth bag and hung away from the dust.

Process

Select good, sound, fresh fruit, but not overripe, or it will be mushy and insipid when cooked. The larger fruits should not be quite as soft for canning as for eating.

Cook in a graniteware or enameled saucepan or preserving kettle. Iron, tin, copper, or brass should not be used.

Always cook slowly, as rapid boiling breaks up the fruit, and causes it to lose much of its nice flavor.

Cook thoroughly and evenly, in small quantities, and in as little water as possible, fruit being better cooked in its own juice, which soon boils out. The length of time required for cooking will depend upon the kind and quantity of fruit, hard and less ripe fruit requiring more time.

Utensils for Canning Fruit

Two or three tablespoonfuls of sugar to each quart of fruit will generally be found sufficient for the milder fruits; the more tart, such as plums, currants, gooseberries, etc., will require from six to eight tablespoonfuls.

While the fruit is cooking, immerse two or three jars in a large pan of scalding (not boiling) water, laying them down if there is room. If the jars are new, put them in cold water, and gradually raise the temperature, to prevent them from breaking. Likewise put the covers in a basin of hot water. Much depends on keeping everything hot.

Have ready an enameled dipper or cup, a cloth for wiping the outside of the jars, a spoon, fork, and a small pan in which to set the jars while being filled.

Utensils for Canning Fruit

When the fruit is well cooked, roll one of the jars over in the hot water, empty it, place it in the small pan, and quickly fill with the boiling fruit, putting in a little of the juice first. Fill to overflowing. Skim off all foam or bubbles of air that come to the top. If any bubbles are seen in the fruit, pass a fork or spoon handle, first dipped in hot water, down into the jar, slightly stirring, when they will come to the top, and can be skimmed off. Wipe the juice from the top of the jar, and screw down the cover quickly and tightly. See that the rubber extends beyond the cover all around. Should any part of the edge of the cover fail to fit down into the rubber tightly after being screwed on, press down all around with the edge of the handle of a strong knife. Turn the jars upside down to cool. If no juice leaks out, the sealing is perfect.

After a few hours turn the jars right side up, and watch for a few days. If there is any leakage or sign of fermentation, the work is a failure, and the fruit should be opened at once, a little more sugar added, boiled, and used as soon as possible. If all is right, store in a cool, dark place for future use. If a proper place is not convenient, wrap the jars in brown paper to keep out the light, as this is likely to cause fermentation.

If the foregoing directions are carefully followed, there is no reason why the work should not be a perfect success.

ANOTHER METHOD

If it is desired to preserve the fruit as nearly whole as possible, prepare it as for cooking, place it, dry, compactly in the jars, and screw the covers on loosely without rubbers. Place the jars, six or eight at a time, in a boiler, standing them on thin pieces of board, and filling the boiler with sufficient warm water to come up half way on the jars. Cover tightly, using a thick cloth, if necessary, to keep in the steam; place on the range, and after the water comes to the boiling-point, cook for from one-half to one hour, according to kind and ripeness of fruit. When cooked, remove the jars, taking care not to allow a draft to strike them, to prevent cracking; allow to settle a few minutes; remove the covers, and fill with a sirup, boiling hot, allowing about a cup of sugar to each quart of fruit; or, if desired to can without sugar, fill the jars with boiling water. Put on the rubbers, and seal at once, testing by turning bottom side up.

Cooking Boiler

This method should be employed in canning vegetables. Only perfectly fresh vegetables should be used for canning.

CANNED BEANS AND PEAS

Prepare string-beans as for ordinary cooking, then press and pack them closely into the jars until full, adding a little salt; fill the jars to overflowing with cold water, then screw on the covers fairly close, place the jars in a boiler, as directed above, and cook for four hours; remove from the water, take off the covers, place on the rubbers, screw on the covers tightly. Peas should be shelled, then canned in the same manner.

CANNED SWEET CORN

Select that which is fresh, and cut from the cob as directed for stewed sweet corn (page 57). Then press and pack closely into the jars until the milk appears on the top, and they are full. No water or salt should be added. Boil for five or six hours.

CANNED PEACHES

Select ripe, firm peaches, nearly soft enough to eat, avoiding the clingstones. The Crawfords are perhaps the best. Pare, divide in halves, removing the stones, and drop into cold water to prevent discoloring. For each quart of fruit pour a cupful of water into a saucepan, add three or four tablespoonfuls of sugar, and let boil up; drain the peaches from the cold water, and put them into the hot sirup; cook slowly till tender, and can.

CANNED BERRIES

Select those freshly picked; if necessary to be washed, place a few at a time in a colander and dip in and out of cold water; cook in a small quantity of water, adding the necessary sugar when nearly done, and can.

CANNED QUINCES

Wipe with a cloth, pare, quarter, core, and divide each quarter into thirds. For each two quarts of fruit pour three cups of water into a saucepan, add nearly two cups of sugar, and let boil up; then put in the fruit, and cook slowly for an hour and a half, or until tender and of a rich pink color, and can. Equal parts of quinces and apples or pears may be stewed together.

CANNED TOMATOES

Select smooth, a little under-ripe, meaty tomatoes; put them into a pan, and pour scalding water over them to make the skins come off readily; then with a sharp, pointed knife remove the cores, pare, cut into thick slices, press well into the jars, screw the covers on loosely without rubbers, place in boiler, and cook for thirty minutes after reaching the boiling-point, according to directions under "Another Method." But little filling will be needed after being cooked. For this have a few tomatoes stewed in a saucepan. Turn upside down till cool, then wrap in brown paper, and keep in a dark place.

GRAPE JUICE

Take fresh, well-ripened, dark, juicy grapes, such as the Black Prince or Concord; pick from the stems, rejecting all that are imperfect; wash well, and put to cook in an enameled saucepan with a pint of water for each three quarts of grapes. Cook slowly for half an hour, or until the grapes burst open; then drain off the juice through a jelly-bag, filtering the skins and seeds through a separate bag. Reheat, add one-half cup of sugar to a quart of juice if desired to sweeten, and can in jars the same as fruit; or, put in sterilized bottles, filling within an inch of the top, and cork at once with good, solid corks; cut off the corks close to the bottle, and seal over with sealing-wax. Bottle the juice from the skins separately, as it will be less clear. Keep in a cool, dark place.

The first wealth is health.—*Emerson.*

Vegetarians suffer little from thirst.—*Hygienic Review.*

Let them give us pulse to eat, and water to drink.—*Daniel.*

Sir Isaac Newton, when writing his great work, "Principia," lived wholly upon a vegetable diet.

Body and mind are much influenced by the kind of food habitually depended upon.—*O. W. Holmes.*

WHILE not furnishing the most nutritious diet, vegetables contain many nutritive elements in moderate degree, are rich in mineral substances, and being composed largely of water, perfectly supply many of the needs of the human system. Such vegetables, however, as peas, beans, and lentils, properly termed legumes, are highly nutritious. They are commonly understood to be of the nature of the "pulse" upon which Daniel the prophet subsisted in preference to the king's meat. While an exclusive diet of ordinary vegetables might fail to give sufficient nourishment to meet the demands of the entire system, their use is valuable in furnishing it with a large quantity of organic fluids, and in giving bulk to the food. It is best to combine their use with other foods, such as grains, which supply the qualities lacking in the vegetables.

Only fresh vegetables should be used. Those which are stale can not be made wholesome and palatable by cooking. Their use imperils the health of the family, and is liable to cause serious illness. Herein lies an advantage in having one's own garden.

Care should be taken not to cook vegetables too much or too little. They should be neither overdone nor underdone, but "just right." Cooking vegetables, grains, and fruits is advantageous, as it bursts the particles of starch, and thus renders them more easy of digestion.

While cooking vegetables, a good, steady fire should be kept up, and the kettle kept full of hot water for replenishing.

Never replenish with cold water, but always with hot.

A good rule to follow in cooking vegetables is to put to cook in hot water all vegetables that require to have the water drained off when done, and in cold water those that are to retain it.

All green vegetables, such as spinach, cabbage, etc., should be put to cook in boiling, salted water; the dry vegetables, such as, potatoes, carrots, beans, split peas, and lentils should be cooked in unsalted water. About a tablespoonful of salt should generally be allowed to a gallon of water, or one third of a teaspoonful to every pint of cooked vegetables.

In washing potatoes, a coarse cloth or brush may be used to advantage. If to be baked, they should be wiped dry before placing in the oven.

It is a matter of both economy and improvement to pare potatoes very thin, as much of the mealiest and most nutritious portion lies next to the skin.

As each potato is pared, it should be dropped into a pan of clean, cold water; if allowed to fall back among the parings, the potatoes will be dark and discolored when cooked.

Potatoes should never be allowed to remain in the water in which they have boiled after they are done. It should be drained off immediately to prevent their becoming soggy and water-soaked. If given a few vigorous shakes, which allows the steam to escape, they will be much more dry and mealy.

Old potatoes, in the spring, should be allowed to stand in cold water for an hour before paring, to reabsorb the moisture they have lost through evaporation.

In baking potatoes the oven should be hot when they are put in, and the temperature increased rather than diminished afterward.

Only dry, ripe, mealy potatoes are good baked.

Onions should be boiled in two waters, first for about fifteen minutes with cold water put on, then drained off, and boiling, salted water added to finish.

To peel tomatoes readily, first pour over them a little scalding water. This also applies to plums.

BOILED POTATOES (without skins)

Saucepan

Wash, pare thin, and drop into cold water to prevent discoloring. If not of a uniform size, cut the larger ones in two. Put to cook in only enough boiling water to prevent burning; cook gently from twenty to thirty minutes; when done, drain off all the water, place over the fire for a moment, then give the saucepan a vigorous shake, cover with a coarse cloth, and set on the back of the range to dry.

Large quantities of potatoes are best cooked by steaming over boiling water.

BOILED POTATOES (with skins)

Select potatoes of even size; wash clean with a cloth or brush, and remove the eyes and specks with a knife; put to cook in a small quantity of boiling water; drain when tender, and place the saucepan on the back of the range to dry; remove the skins and serve. Potatoes are best cooked in this way. Serve in an open vegetable dish.

BAKED POTATOES

Choose smooth potatoes of uniform size, wash well, being careful to clean the eyes. Dry with a cloth, and bake in a *hot* oven; in a slow oven the skins become thick and hard. Serve as soon as done, in an open dish; if covered, they will become soggy. Baked potatoes are very wholesome, and make a good breakfast dish.

MASHED POTATOES

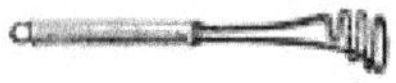

Potato Masher

Wash, pare, and boil the same as boiled potatoes. When they can be readily pierced with a fork, drain thoroughly; return to the range and mash, using the potato masher vigorously for five or ten minutes, until they are light, smooth, and creamy in appearance. A wire potato masher does the work most satisfactorily. Have warmed in a saucepan a half cupful of cream or milk, adding a small piece of butter if milk is used, a teaspoonful of salt, and the well-beaten white of one egg; beat this into the potatoes until they are very light. Put lightly into a warm dish, but do not press down, and serve at once. If desired, the egg may be omitted. Very nice served with cream sauce or brown sauce.

STEAMED SLICED POTATOES

Wash, pare, and slice several medium-sized potatoes very thin. Have in a frying-pan a small piece of butter and a half cup of hot water, put in the potatoes, season with salt, cover closely, and set on the back of the range to cook slowly. Stir up a little occasionally. A few thinly sliced onions may be used with the potatoes if desired.

WARMED-UP POTATOES

Cut cold boiled potatoes into thin slices; heat a little milk to boiling in a saucepan; put in the potatoes, and season with salt to taste. Let boil a few minutes and serve. If desired, the milk may be slightly thickened with a little flour blended in a little cold milk.

POTATO PUFF

Take two cupfuls of hot, seasoned, mashed potatoes, and moisten well with hot milk or cream. Beat the yolks and whites of two eggs separately; allow the potatoes to cool slightly, then beat in the eggs, the yolks first. Turn at once into an oiled, shallow tin; do not smooth or press them down, but leave in a rocky form. Bake about ten minutes, or till a delicate brown.

LYONNAISE POTATOES

Cut into dice enough cold boiled potatoes to make one pint, brown to a golden yellow a spoonful each of butter or oil and minced onion. Add the potatoes, season with salt, and stir with a fork till a delicate brown, being careful not to break them. Add a spoonful of chopped parsley, and serve hot.

NEW POTATOES

If new and fresh, the skins may be easily scraped off with a knife, or rubbed off with a coarse cloth. Cook in a little water, drain, and serve; or, when done, drain, pour some rich, sweet milk over them, let it heat to boiling, then thicken with a little flour rubbed smooth in a little cold milk, allowing a tablespoonful of flour to a pint of milk, and season with salt. A few green peas cooked with new potatoes and thus dressed make a very acceptable dish.

POTATOES WITH CREAM

Pare, and cut as many as desired into small cubes; put into boiling water and cook from fifteen to twenty minutes; when done, drain off all the water, let dry a few minutes over the fire, then add a little salt, a cup of thin cream, and a little chopped parsley; simmer for two or three minutes, and serve at once.

BAKED SWEET POTATOES

Choose those of uniform size, wash thoroughly, removing any imperfect spots, wipe dry, and place in a moderately hot oven; bake for about an hour if the potatoes are rather large. Small potatoes are better steamed than baked. Send to the table as soon as done, after removing the skins.

BOILED SWEET POTATOES

Wash well, put into cold water with the skins on, and boil until easily pierced with a fork; drain, remove the skins, and place in the oven to dry for five or ten minutes; serve in a hot, open dish.

BROWNED SWEET POTATOES

Take cold, boiled sweet potatoes, peel, cut into halves, place on shallow buttered tins, and brown in a hot oven.

ROASTED SWEET POTATOES

Wash, wipe dry, wrap with thin paper, and cover first with hot ashes, then with live coals. Turn occasionally. The coals may need renewing several times. When done, remove the ashes with a brush, wipe with a dry cloth, and serve. Sweet potatoes are nicer and more mealy when prepared in this way.

YAMS

Prepare the same as roasted sweet potatoes or baked sweet potatoes. Boiling them is thought to quite spoil their flavor.

STEWED TOMATOES

Take nice, fresh tomatoes, pour boiling water over them, remove the skins, slice into a granite saucepan, add a cupful of water, and stew from twenty to thirty minutes. Then add salt, butter, and a half cup of bread or cracker crumbs, or slightly thicken with cornstarch, blended with a little cold water. Sugar may be added if desired.

BAKED TOMATOES

Select smooth, even-sized, ripe tomatoes. Peel, remove the stems, and place in an earthen pudding dish; season with a little salt and butter or cream, and bake in a rather hot oven for half an hour.

TOMATOES AND MACARONI

Put to cook one-half cup of macaroni broken into inch pieces into three cups of boiling water; boil for about an hour, or until perfectly tender, adding more water if necessary. When done, put into a pudding dish, and pour over two cups of stewed tomatoes previously rubbed through a colander. Add a little salt, a few bits of butter, a half cup of sweet cream, and bake in the oven till done. If the tomatoes are quite juicy, a teaspoonful of flour may be used for thickening.

Colander

SCALLOPED TOMATOES

Can Opener.

Take one quart of stewed fresh or canned tomatoes, rub through a colander, and thicken with a cupful of bread or cracker crumbs; add a little salt, a few spoonfuls of cream, and bake for twenty or thirty minutes.

BOILED BEANS

Pick over, wash, and soak two cupfuls of beans overnight in cold water. In the morning drain, and put to cook in hot water. Cook slowly for two or three hours, or until perfectly tender, adding more hot water as needed, as they should be quite juicy when done; avoid much stirring. Season with salt and a little butter or cream. Colored beans having too strong a flavor may be improved by parboiling for fifteen minutes, then draining, and putting to cook in fresh boiling water.

BOILED BEANS WITH RICE

Wash and soak two cupfuls of beans in cold water overnight; in the morning put to cook, and after about an hour add one-half cup of well-washed rice. Cook slowly until done, season as above, and serve.

BAKED BEANS

Take two cupfuls of beans, pick over, wash, soak overnight, and cook the same as boiled beans. When done, add a little butter and salt, and two tablespoonfuls of molasses; turn into a pudding dish, and bake until nicely browned. A little hot water should be added occasionally to prevent their becoming too dry.

BAKED GREEN BEANS AND CORN

Shell the beans, and cut the sweet corn from the cob. Put layers of each in equal quantities in a bean pot or pan, seasoning with salt and butter. Add boiling water to cover, and bake in the oven for about two hours, adding more hot water as it becomes absorbed.

MASHED BEANS

Soak overnight two cupfuls of beans, and cook the same as boiled beans. When very tender, and the water nearly absorbed, rub through a colander to remove the skins; add half a cup of cream or of rich, sweet milk and a little butter; put into a shallow dish, smooth the top with a knife or spoon, and place in the oven to brown.

STRING BEANS

Wash, break off each end, stripping the strong fibers from end to end. Cut or break into inch lengths, and put to cook in enough boiling, slightly salted water to cover. Cook from one to two hours, or until very tender, the length of time required depending upon the age and variety of the beans. The water should be quite absorbed when done. Add a little milk and butter if cream is not available. Let come to a boil, and serve.

SPLIT PEAS

Look over carefully, wash, and put to cook in a good quantity of cold water. Let come to a boil, then simmer until tender and the water quite absorbed. Press through a colander if desired to remove the skins, season with salt, and cream or butter, and serve.

GREEN PEAS

Shell, and put to cook in boiling, slightly salted water, allowing one cupful of water to every four cups of peas. If they are old, and need longer cooking, add more water if necessary. Cover, and cook rather slowly till tender. About thirty minutes' cooking for fresh, young peas will be found sufficient. When done, pour over a cupful of sweet milk, heat to boiling, and thicken with a little flour. Season with a little salt, and a spoonful of cream or a small piece of butter.

LENTILS

Cook, season, and serve the same as split peas, only less water and less time for cooking will be required.

BAKED RICE

Take one cupful of rice, wash well by turning into a colander and dipping in and out of warm water, put into a pudding dish, and pour over four cupfuls of milk, or two each of milk and water, adding a little salt. Bake about an hour, stirring once or twice before the top becomes hard. Serve as a vegetable with lentil sauce.

PLAIN BOILED RICE

Wash thoroughly one cupful of rice, and sprinkle it slowly into a granite saucepan containing two or three quarts of rapidly boiling, slightly salted water. If the grains sink to the bottom, stir gently until they keep in motion themselves. Boil rapidly, without covering, for thirty minutes, or until soft; then drain through a colander and rinse with hot water to remove all starch. The grains should be separate and distinct from one another. It may be served with a tomato sauce. See page 77.

SPAGHETTI WITH TOMATO SAUCE

Break in pieces and cook in boiling, salted water, or cook whole by dipping the ends in the hot water, and as they bend, coil them around in the saucepan. Cook for twenty or thirty minutes, or until soft, then drain, rinse with hot water to remove starch if it is sticky, turn into a dish and pour over a hot tomato sauce, made as directed on page 77.

STEWED CAULIFLOWER

Carefully separate into small portions; examine closely to make sure there are no insects on it; let stand a short time in cold water, then put into boiling, salted water, and cook from twenty to forty minutes, or until tender. Drain, season with a little butter or cream, or serve with cream sauce poured over it.

CAULIFLOWER WITH TOMATO SAUCE

Cook the same as stewed cauliflower. When done, drain, turn into a dish, and pour over it a hot tomato sauce.

STEWED CABBAGE

Remove the outer leaves, divide into halves, cut very fine with a sharp knife, omitting the heart. Put into a saucepan with a half cup of boiling water, add a little salt, cover closely, and cook until tender, adding a little more hot water, if it becomes too dry before it is done. When done, add a few spoonfuls of cream, allow to heat, and serve.

BOILED CABBAGE

Remove the outer leaves, place in cold water for half an hour, then quarter, and put to cook in boiling water, adding a little salt. Boil vigorously for about thirty minutes; turn into a colander, remove the heart and coarse portions, press out all the water, return to the saucepan, and season with butter or cream; allow to heat, and serve on a hot dish at once.

BOILED CELERY

Take one bunch of celery, cut off tops and roots, scrape and wash the stalks, then cut them into small pieces, and put to cook in boiling water. Let cook for fifteen or twenty minutes, or until tender; drain, turn into a heated dish, and pour over a cream sauce. For making cream sauce see page 77.

STEWED ASPARAGUS

Wash, break into small pieces, and cook from twenty to thirty minutes in just enough water to cover; when tender, drain, add a little butter and salt and a cup of milk; let come to a boil, and thicken with a teaspoonful of flour. Boil up and serve.

BOILED CARROTS

Select small or medium-sized carrots, wash, scrape, rinse in cold water, then put to cook in boiling water; cook about thirty minutes, or until tender, then drain. Serve as boiled, or slice them into a heated vegetable dish, and pour over them a cream sauce prepared as directed on page 77.

BOILED PARSNIPS

Prepare and cook the same as boiled carrots.

BAKED PARSNIPS

Wash, scrape, rinse, divide in halves, add a little more than enough boiling water to cook them, and boil slowly until tender; place in a shallow dish, pour over the juice that remains, add a little salt, a spoonful or two of cream, and place in the oven until nicely browned, basting occasionally.

STEWED TURNIPS

Pare the turnips, cut into slices, and cook until perfectly tender; then drain, mash fine with a spoon or potato masher, season with salt, a little butter or cream if desired, and serve.

SLICED CUCUMBERS

Pare the cucumbers, slice them very thin into a dish, sprinkle with salt, cover loosely, and shake briskly to distribute the salt; let stand for about half an hour; then drain off all the water, and shortly before serving pour over the juice of one or two lemons. A spoonful or two of cream may be added if desired. Cucumbers should be thoroughly masticated. Their reputed indigestibility is largely due to a failure in this particular.

BOILED ONIONS

Cut off the tops and bottoms, remove the outer skins, and put to cook in cold water; boil fifteen minutes; then drain, and cook in boiling, salted water until tender; turn into a pudding dish, and cut into small pieces; pour over a cupful of hot cream sauce, sprinkle the top with bread crumbs, and bake until brown. For making cream sauce see page 77.

BAKED SQUASH

Cut into sections, and place shell downward on the top shelf of the oven. Bake until tender, and serve hot in the shell; or, scrape out the inside, mash, add a few spoonfuls of cream or a little butter, and serve.

STEWED SQUASH

Peel, remove seeds, cut into small pieces, and stew until tender in a little boiling water; drain, mash smooth, and season with butter and salt. Vegetable marrows may be prepared in the same manner.

SUCCOTASH

Soak one cupful of beans overnight. When ready to cook, add water and one cupful of dried sweet corn, and cook until tender. Season with salt, a little cream or butter, and serve. If green sweet corn is used, do not add it to the beans until they are nearly done.

BOILED SWEET CORN

Select full-grown ears, not old and hard, but full of milk; remove the husks and silks, and put to cook in enough boiling, salted water to cover. Boil from thirty to forty minutes; when done, drain, and serve on the cob hot, with a little butter if desired. The corn from ears not eaten may be cut from the cob and warmed up with a little cream or butter for the next meal.

STEWED SWEET CORN

Remove husks and silks, stand the ears in a dish, and with a sharp knife cut off the corn from the top downward, taking a little more than half of the kernel in depth; then scrape gently downward to get the remainder of the milk and meat of each kernel. Place in a saucepan, add half a cup of water for each quart of corn, and cook for fifteen or twenty minutes. When done, add a little salt, a half cup of cream, or a cup of milk and a little butter, boil up and serve. The milk may be slightly thickened with flour, if desired.

BAKED BEETS

Take young, tender beets, wash clean, place in a baking dish with a little water, and bake from one to two hours, or until tender; add a little hot water occasionally if they become dry. When done, remove the skins, slice, and serve with lemon-juice.

BOILED BEETS

Cut off the tops, but avoid cutting the beets; put to cook in boiling water. When tender, remove to a pan of cold water; rub off the skins with the hands, slice thin, and serve with lemon-juice.

BEET GREENS

Take the tops from young, tender beets, look over, put to cook in boiling, slightly salted water, and cook until tender; then drain in a colander; chop rather fine, and serve with lemon-juice.

SPINACH

Look over carefully a good quantity of spinach, rejecting all wilted and decayed leaves. Wash thoroughly in several waters, and put to cook in slightly salted, boiling water, and boil from twenty to thirty minutes. When tender, drain in a colander, cut into coarse pieces, and put into a warm dish; add a few bits of butter, and garnish with slices of hard-boiled eggs. Serve with lemon-juice.

CELERY

Remove all the green and decayed parts from the stalks, and put into cold water. When ready to serve, place in a celery glass with the small ends downward. Curl the tops by cutting into narrow strips a little way down. Celery is recommended as a good nerve food.

Plain and healthful living tends to long and happy living.—*Selected.*

The foundation of a happy home is laid in the kitchen.—*Marion Harland.*

TOMATO SALAD, NO. 1

Peel smooth, ripe tomatoes, cut into thin slices, and arrange in layers in a dish, sprinkling each layer with sugar. Turn over the whole a half cup of lemon-juice before serving.

TOMATO SALAD, NO. 2

Peel, slice, and place in a dish, and sprinkle lightly with salt. To the beaten yolk of one egg add the juice of one or two lemons, a teaspoonful of sugar, and pour all together over the tomatoes.

CABBAGE SALAD, NO. 1

Chop very fine half a small head of crisp cabbage, and put into a dish. Mix together two tablespoonfuls of sugar and the juice of two lemons, and pour over the cabbage; add a spoonful or two of thick cream, stir together, and serve. The cream may be omitted if preferred.

CABBAGE SALAD, NO. 2

Chop the cabbage fine, and dress with mayonnaise dressing. If preferred omit to thin the dressing with cream, and cover the cabbage with whipped cream, slightly sweetened.

CABBAGE AND TOMATO SALAD

Cut the cabbage as above, and put into a dish. Peel and slice two or three large, ripe tomatoes, and place on the cabbage. Toss up lightly in the dish, sprinkle with sugar, and pour over all the juice of two lemons.

LETTUCE SALAD, NO. 1

Separate the leaves, look over, wash, and put into cold water a while before using. When ready to serve, place on a dish and pour over a dressing made of equal quantities of lemon-juice, sugar, and water.

LETTUCE SALAD, NO. 2

Wash and shred two heads of lettuce. Boil two eggs until hard, remove the shells, and mash the yolks fine; mix well together the juice of one or two lemons, two or three tablespoonfuls of water, one tablespoonful of sugar, one-half teaspoonful of salt, one tablespoonful of sweet cream, adding this last to prevent curdling, and the yolks of the eggs, and pour over the lettuce. Cut the whites of the eggs into rings and arrange on the top. A spoonful or two of minced onion may also be added.

POTATO SALAD

Cut into thin slices, hot or cold boiled potatoes, and place in a dish without breaking slices. A small onion, chopped fine, to each pint of potatoes may be added if desired. Cover with mayonnaise dressing.

VEGETABLE SALAD

Put a layer of fresh watercress or lettuce into a salad bowl, then alternate with layers of peeled, thinly sliced cucumber and tomatoes. When enough is prepared, place a border of watercress around the bowl. Just before serving, pour over a French dressing, and toss up lightly with a fork till well mingled.

FRUIT SALAD

Place in salad dish alternate layers of sliced bananas and strawberries, sprinkling each layer with sugar. Cover with whipped cream, and serve.

BANANA SALAD

Slice crosswise six ripe bananas into a dish; sprinkle with powdered sugar, then turn over them the juice of two nice large oranges; let stand for an hour in a cool place, and serve.

NUT AND CELERY SALAD

Take three cupfuls of finely cut, crisp celery, and one cupful of chopped English walnuts; dress with mayonnaise dressing, made thin with a little sweet cream.

FRENCH DRESSING

Mix thoroughly together six tablespoonfuls of oil, a pinch of salt, and two tablespoonfuls of lemon-juice.

MAYONNAISE DRESSING

To the yolks of two fresh eggs add a scant teaspoonful of salt; then beat in slowly, almost drop by drop, a small cupful of olive-oil. The mixture should become nearly as thick as butter. Then gradually add one tablespoonful of lemon-juice. Thin with sweet cream. Nice for potato, cabbage, or nut salads. If used for tomato salad, omit the cream.

As a man eateth, so is he.—*German Proverb.*

Lord Byron refused to eat meat because, as he said, "It makes me ferocious."

The flesh of animals tends to cause grossness of body, and to benumb the finer sensibilities of the mind.—"*Bible Hygiene.*"

The eating of much flesh fills us with a multitude of evil diseases, and a multitude of evil desires. —*Porphyrises, 233* A. D.

Animal food is one of the greatest means by which the pure sentiment of the race is depressed.—*Alcott.*

The candidates for ancient athletic games were dieted on boiled grain with warm water, cheese, and dried figs, but no meat. Modern athletes are not allowed meat while in training.

I have known men who prayed for a good temper in vain, until their physician proscribed eating so much meat; for they could not endure such stimulation.—*Henry Ward Beecher.*

The liability to disease is increased by flesh eating. Where plenty of good milk and fruit can be obtained, there is rarely any excuse for eating animal food.—"*Christian Temperance.*"

FROM the instruction given at the beginning respecting foods, it is evident the Creator did not design that either man or beast should subsist on flesh foods. To Adam and Eve he said: "Behold, I have given you every herb bearing seed, which is upon the face of all the earth, and every tree, in the which is the fruit of a tree yielding seed; to you it shall be for meat. And to every beast of the earth, and to every fowl of the air, and to everything that creepeth upon the earth, wherein there is life, I have given every green herb for meat." Gen. 1:29, 30.

But sin brought many changes into our world, and because of the changed circumstances, customs, and practises were instituted and allowed which were not in harmony with the primeval order of things. Among other things meat eating was permitted. Just after the flood, when the face of the earth had been desolated, God said to Noah: “Every moving thing that liveth shall be meat for you; even as the green herb have I given you all things.” Gen. 9:3. But the blood was not to be eaten with the flesh,—a very wise provision, for if there is any disease in the system, it is sure to be found in the blood.

A little later, as a further precaution in the interests of health, instruction was given that only the flesh of “clean beasts” was to be eaten, such as that of the ox, the sheep, the goat, the deer, etc. See Leviticus 11 and Deuteronomy 14.

But for all this it must be admitted that the flesh of animals is not a natural diet for man, nor does it constitute the most healthful food. Of this it may be truly said as Christ said of the granting of a writing of divorcement, it was suffered because of the “hardness” of their hearts, “but from the beginning it was not so.” Matt. 19:8. It was never intended that man should take the life of any innocent, living creature.

Meat eating tends to excite the passions. This is seen in the animal kingdom. The animals that are mild, patient, and docile are generally herbivorous, such as the cow, the sheep, the horse; while the excitable, quick-tempered, and ferocious animals are meat eaters, such as the lion, the tiger, the leopard. A meat diet also tends to constipation, the great scourge of the race.

One object of this work, therefore, is in the interests of health and morality, to educate people out of meat eating rather than into it; and to supply such a variety of recipes for good, wholesome, palatable, and nutritious dishes, prepared from natural food elements, that meat eating will be practically unnecessary.

Moreover, so many animals at the present time are becoming so greatly diseased that it is not a little dangerous to eat largely of their flesh. As a matter of safety the use of flesh-meats might very consistently be dispensed with altogether.

The fact, therefore, that meat may be cheap, or that it may be easily or quickly prepared, should count for little with those who have the best interests of their families in view.

From every standpoint from which the subject may be viewed, the reasons for discontinuing the use of flesh-meats are more imperative now than ever before.

1. This is an age of disease. Animals are coming to be greatly diseased. The use of their flesh, therefore, tends to increase disease in mankind, and thus to shorten life.

2. This is an age of intemperance. Flesh-meats are all more or less stimulating. Their use, therefore, tends to increase this evil.

3. This is an age of surfeiting. Meat eating is, to a large degree, responsible for this. A well-known English writer on cookery says: "No one will deny that the foods we are apt to eat too much of are those absent from a purely vegetarian fare, such as meat, game, fish, eggs, etc., upon which materials the culinary art seems exercised to tempt us beyond the satisfying of the appetite."

4. This is an age of vice and immorality. A meat diet tends greatly to increase this terrible evil.

5. This is an age of violence and murder. The practise of killing and eating animals tends to harden men's hearts, to destroy their finer sensibilities, and thus to increase violence and crime.

In the beginning God gave man no flesh foods to eat. And after the Exodus, when he had his own way with his own people, he gave them no flesh to eat. Before taking them into the promised land, for forty years he fed them on "manna," a purely vegetarian food. Ex. 16:31; Num. 11:7, 8. And when they "fell a lusting," and said, "Who shall give us flesh to eat?" he was displeased with them, and, with the giving of the quails, brought a great plague upon them. Numbers 11; Ps. 78:18-31.

In the New Testament, the apostle, referring to this experience, warns Christians against falling into the same error. "Now these things," he says, "were our examples, to the intent we should not lust after evil things, as they also lusted.... And they are written for our admonition, upon whom the ends of the world are come.” 1 Cor. 10:5-11.

Evidently, therefore, meat eating is not in harmony with God’s original plan. And it must be that the nearer we bring ourselves into harmony with that plan, the better it will be for us.

To some it may seem difficult to give up the use of meat. But in this, as in all reformatory work, much depends upon the mind. Let the correct principle be first assented to; then, step by step, let the practise be brought into conformity to the principle, making changes gradually, if necessary, leaving off the meat dishes as others more wholesome can be substituted. We should cultivate a love for that which we know to be good and healthful.

To assist those who desire to make this dietetic reform, a few recipes are here given which will be found to be good substitutes for meats.

VEGETABLE AND LENTIL STEW

Soak one-half cup of lentils in a cup of cold water for an hour; then put to cook in three cups of hot water with one turnip, three or four medium-sized potatoes, a small onion, and a stalk or two of celery, all cut into small pieces. Stew for about half an hour, or until well done, and the water quite absorbed. Season with salt, and serve with brown sauce.

VEGETABLE HASH

Boil separately in a small quantity of water, three or four medium-sized potatoes sliced fine, two turnips, one carrot, and an onion, all cut into fine pieces; when done, drain, and turn all together into a saucepan; season with salt, add a teaspoonful of dry, powdered sage, a half cup of sweet cream, or the same quantity of milk, and a small piece of butter, and heat to boiling; then stir in one or two tablespoonfuls of browned flour rubbed to a paste in a little cold water, cook a few minutes longer, and serve hot.

POTATO ROLLS

Take two potatoes, one turnip, a small onion, a stalk of celery, and a little powdered sage; chop all into very fine pieces and mix well together, adding salt as desired. Make a paste as for pies, roll out rather thin, cut into squares, and place on each square as much of the mixture as it will hold; wet the edges, and fold up as a sausage roll, pressing the dough together at the ends, place in a pan and bake from thirty to forty minutes in a moderate oven. Serve hot. Very nice.

BREAD STEAK

Dip slices of stale bread or toast in a little milk or cream to slightly soften; sprinkle with a little salt; beat up an egg or two, dip in the slices, place in a hot frying-pan with a little butter, and brown on both sides. Serve with brown sauce.

FORCEMEAT FRITTERS

Rub one tablespoonful of butter into two cupfuls of fine breads crumbs, adding a little chopped parsley or other herb flavoring, and season with salt; then add one cup of thin cream or rich milk, and three eggs beaten separately. Stir well, and bake in fritters, in a hot frying-pan, or on a griddle, rubbed with a little butter, browning lightly on both sides. Serve with brown sauce.

"PRAIRIE" FISH

Cut thick, cold, corn-meal mush into slices about half an inch thick; roll in flour, and brown on both sides in a hot, buttered frying-pan; or brush with thick, sweet cream, and brown in the oven.

BOILED MACARONI

If dusty, wipe with a dry cloth instead of washing, then take a cupful broken into small pieces, and put to cook in boiling, salted water; cook until tender, adding more hot water occasionally if necessary. When done, drain, and serve hot with a little cream; or pour over a pint of milk, heat to boiling, and stir in the yolk of one well-beaten egg and a little salt; or omit the egg, and thicken with a tablespoonful of flour rubbed smooth in a little cold milk.

PEANUT SAUSAGE

Thoroughly mix to a cream one level tablespoonful of peanut butter with two tablespoonfuls of cold water; then add three tablespoonfuls of grated bread crumbs, a pinch of salt, and a teaspoonful of minced onion or powdered sage; mix all well together, form into small cakes with the hands, and place in an oiled, heated frying-pan till nicely browned, turning and browning on both sides. Place on a platter, and garnish with sprigs of parsley. Serve with brown sauce, No. 2, page 78. Very tasty.

PEAS PUREE

Soak a cupful or two, or as many as needed, of split peas overnight in cold water. In the morning wash, drain, and put to cook in boiling water, and cook slowly. When very tender, and quite dry, mash smooth, season with salt and a little sweet cream. Serve hot.

STEWED SALSIFY, OR VEGETABLE OYSTERS

Wash, scrape, cut into slices about one fourth of an inch in thickness, and drop at once into cold water to prevent discoloring. Then put to cook in an enameled saucepan, in a small quantity of boiling water, about equal parts of water and salsify, adding a little salt. Cook from twenty to fifty minutes, according to age, and when tender add a little more water if at all dry, a cupful of cream or rich milk, and simmer for a few minutes. Have ready in a dish some slices of toasted bread cut in halves, pour over the salsify, and serve.

LENTIL RISSOLES

Take equal quantities of well-cooked brown lentils and cold boiled potatoes and mash well together; then add one third that amount of fine bread crumbs, a teaspoonful each of powdered sage and minced onion, and a little salt. Dissolve a teaspoonful of nut butter in two tablespoonfuls of hot water; and add to the mixture. Mix all well together, press into an oiled tin, cut into squares with a knife, and place in the oven for fifteen or twenty minutes. Serve hot.

Food should be prepared with simplicity, yet with a nicety which will invite the appetite.

There should not be many kinds at any one meal, but all meals should not be composed of the same kinds of food without variation.

The mother should study to set a simple yet nutritious diet before her family.—*Mrs. E. G. White.*

BOILED EGGS

If desired to have the white set, but the yolk a liquid, boil eggs three minutes; then remove from the fire and leave them in the hot water a moment or two to set the whites. The water should be boiling when the eggs are dropped in.

If desired to have the yolks dry and mealy, and at the same time the whites not hard, tough, and leathery, place the eggs in boiling water, then let simmer in water a little below the boiling-point, or at a temperature not above 165° Fahrenheit, for about twenty minutes. Eggs are best cooked thus.

For garnishing salads, etc., boil about twenty minutes, then immediately place a moment in cold water to prevent the whites becoming discolored, and to make the shells remove easily.

POACHED EGGS

Put into a shallow pan as much hot water as will cover the eggs well. A tablespoonful of lemon-juice may be added to the water to make the eggs white. Break the eggs one at a time into a cup and slip gently into the water, which should not boil, but only simmer. Let stand for about five minutes, or until the white is firm, but not hard, and the yolk enveloped in a film of white. Remove each egg with a skimmer, or large spoon, drain, trim the edges, and serve in egg saucers, or on toast. Make a thin cream sauce and pour around them if desired.

SCRAMBLED EGGS

For each egg allow two tablespoonfuls of boiling water or milk. Break the eggs into a dish, beat lightly with a spoon, add a little salt, drop into the boiling water or milk, and stir briskly until set, but soft. They are nice thus served on toast.

STEAMED EGGS

Break the eggs into egg dishes or oiled patty-pans, sprinkle with salt, and steam over boiling water until the whites are set and a film covers the yolk. Serve with or without toast.

SCALLOPED EGGS

Boil five or six eggs for twenty minutes; remove the shells, and cut the eggs into thin slices; put a layer of grated or fine bread crumbs into a buttered pudding dish, then a layer of the sliced eggs; sprinkle with salt, then add another layer of bread crumbs, then another of egg, and so on till the dish is filled, having a layer of crumbs for the top. Heat a cup of milk to boiling, and pour over the scallop; sprinkle over a few more crumbs, and bake until slightly browned.

BAKED EGGS

Break the required number of eggs into a shallow baking pan, or small patty-pans, previously buttered, to prevent sticking. Season with salt, and bake until set. Remove to a warm platter, and serve at once.

EGG SANDWICHES

Mash the yolks of two hard-boiled eggs, a sprinkle of salt, and a little chopped cress, smooth and fine; spread this on thin slices of bread slightly buttered, and press together.

EGGS AND TOMATO SAUCE

Melt a spoonful of butter in a deep dish, break in carefully the number of eggs desired, and place on the stove until they begin to set; then pour over them a hot tomato sauce, made after directions on page 77.

EGGS ON TOAST

Boil three eggs for twenty minutes. Put one tablespoonful of butter into a frying-pan. When hot, stir in one tablespoonful of flour, one-fourth teaspoonful of salt, and gradually, to avoid lumps forming, one cupful of milk. Add the whites of the three eggs, chopped fine. When hot, pour over three or four slices of moistened toast. Put the yolks through a sieve or vegetable press over the toast, garnish with bits of parsley, and serve hot.

Simple diet is best; for many dishes bring many diseases.—*Pliny.*

PLAIN OMELET

Beat the yolks and whites of three eggs separately; allow one tablespoonful of milk to each egg. Stir the milk and yolks of the eggs well together and season with salt; then with a spoon carefully fold in the stiffly beaten whites of the eggs. Turn all into a hot frying-pan, sufficiently buttered to prevent sticking. Cook rather quickly, being careful not to burn. Carefully lift the edges of the omelet while cooking, with a knife or spoon, that it may be equally cooked. When well set, double one part over the other, remove to a warm dish, and serve at once, as an omelet is not so good when cold. It should be very light and tender, and nicely browned.

FRUIT OMELET

Prepare as above, spreading a thin layer of any kind of jelly over one half before folding the other half over it; add a sprinkle of sugar if desired.

BREAD OMELET

For each person allow one egg, three tablespoonfuls of milk, and one tablespoonful of finely grated bread crumbs; beat well together, and add a little salt, butter a deep plate or shallow pan, pour in the mixture, and bake in the oven until well set.

MACARONI OMELET

Take a small handful of macaroni broken into small pieces, drop into hot water, and boil until tender; drain. Heat a cupful of milk to boiling, and stir in two even tablespoonfuls of flour rubbed smooth in a little cold milk. Stir until thickened; remove from the fire, add the macaroni, a few bits of chopped parsley, and four eggs well beaten; season with salt; pour all into a hot, buttered dish, sprinkle with a small handful of bread crumbs, and place in the oven till nicely browned; then turn out on a hot, flat dish, and serve with brown sauce.

The proof of the pudding is in eating it.

Eat to live, but do not live merely to eat.

Health is the greatest of all possessions, and 'tis a maxim with me, that a hale cobbler is better than a sick king.—*Bicherstaff.*

In order to preserve health, temperance in all things is necessary—temperance in labor, temperance in eating and drinking.—*"Christian Temperance."*

SAGO PUDDING

To five cups of boiling water add a cup of sago, previously soaked in a cup of cold water for twenty minutes, two thirds of a cup of sugar, and a half cup of well-washed raisins. Cook all together till transparent, flavor with lemon or vanilla, and serve with cream or boiled custard sauce.

TAPIOCA PUDDING

Soak one cupful of tapioca overnight in a pint of water. In the morning add one quart of milk, stirring gently, and boil about twenty minutes; then add the yolks of four eggs well beaten, and one cup of sugar, and boil a few minutes longer; pour into an earthen dish, and flavor with a teaspoonful of vanilla; cover with a meringue made of the whites of the four eggs beaten stiff, and four tablespoonfuls of powdered sugar, and place in a slow oven to brown slightly. Serve cold.

RICE PUDDING

Take a cupful of boiled rice, and a half cup of washed raisins, and mix together in a pudding dish. Beat well together two eggs, two tablespoonfuls of sugar, and two cupfuls of milk, and pour over the raisins and rice. Bake in a moderate oven until the custard is just set. If left in too long, the milk becomes watery. This is a good way to use up left-over rice.

CORNSTARCH PUDDING

Take three tablespoonfuls of cornstarch and stir smooth in a little cold water; over this pour one pint of boiling water; then stir in the whites of three eggs beaten stiff, one tablespoonful of sugar, and a pinch of salt. Steam fifteen minutes, or cook slowly until thickened. Serve cold with a sauce prepared as follows: Heat one cup of milk to boiling; beat together the yolks of the three eggs and one-half cup of sugar until creamy, and stir into the milk; boil until smooth, and remove from the fire at once. Flavor with lemon or vanilla, and allow to cool.

BREAD PUDDING, NO. 1

Take one pint of bread crumbs, and pour over them one quart of milk; then add the yolks of four eggs well beaten, four tablespoonfuls of sugar, and bake in the oven. When done, spread the top with jelly or marmalade, and cover with a meringue made of the four whites of the eggs beaten stiff, and two tablespoonfuls of powdered sugar. Brown slightly, and serve warm or cold, with or without sauce or cream, as preferred.

BREAD PUDDING, NO. 2

Cut stale bread into cubes, and moisten with milk or water; then pour over a mixture of eggs, sugar, and milk, allowing one egg and one tablespoonful of sugar to each cup of milk. Steam or bake. Currants or raisins may be added.

COLD PEACH PUDDING

Cut slices of stale bread into strips, and line a pudding basin or round mold as neatly as possible. Then fill the center of the mold with stewed fresh or canned peaches, slightly warmed, add sugar to sweeten, and place a slice of bread over the fruit. Pour over enough of the sirup or fruit juice to soak all the bread. Take a saucer or plate about the size of the mold, and place it upside down on top, over the pudding, and put a heavy weight on the plate. Let stand overnight, and in the morning turn into a glass dish for the table. Cut into slices, and serve with milk or cream. Raspberries or blackberries may be used instead of peaches.

PRUNE WHIP

Wash thoroughly one-half pound of prunes and soak for an hour in cold water enough to cover; cook gently in the same water until the prunes are tender, and the juice is nearly absorbed. Then rub through a colander. When cold, add two tablespoonfuls of sugar, a little lemon-juice, and the stiffly beaten whites of three eggs. Stir all well together, pile lightly in a buttered pudding dish, and bake about ten minutes, or until a delicate brown. Serve with whipped cream or boiled custard sauce. See pages 79 and 78.

FIG PUDDING

Take half a pound of finely chopped figs, one cupful of bread crumbs, three tablespoonfuls of sugar, two tablespoonfuls of melted butter, one cupful of milk, two eggs well beaten, and a pinch of salt. Stir all well together, turn into a double boiler, slightly buttered, or into a saucepan placed in boiling water, and boil about an hour. Serve with lemon sauce.

RICE LEMON PUDDING

To three-fourths cupful of well-washed rice, add three cupfuls of boiling water and a half teaspoonful of salt, and cook in a double boiler until tender. When done, allow to cool, then add the yolks of three eggs well beaten, a teaspoonful of butter, three tablespoonfuls of sugar, the grated rind of a lemon, and one cup of milk; stir together, and bake in the oven until set. When done, cover the top with a meringue made with the whites of the eggs beaten stiff, two-thirds cup of sugar, and the juice of one lemon; place in the oven to brown slightly. Serve either warm or cold.

RICE APPLE PUDDING

Boil two tablespoonfuls of well-washed rice in half a pint of milk until soft; then stir in the beaten yolks of two eggs and sugar to sweeten. Make a wall with the rice around a dish; fill the center of the dish with stewed apples, and cover the whole with the whites of the eggs beaten to a stiff froth; sprinkle with powdered sugar, and brown lightly in the oven; serve with plain or whipped cream.

CRACKER PUDDING

Put three cupfuls of rich milk into a pudding dish; sprinkle in two cupfuls of crackers, first heated in the oven till crisp, but not browned, and afterward crushed fine with a rolling-pin. Beat the yolks of three eggs till light; then mix with one-half cup of sugar, and stir in the crackers and milk; add one cup of well-washed currants or seedless raisins, and flavor with grated lemon peel if desired. Bake in the oven until set; beat the whites of the eggs till stiff, add one tablespoonful of white sugar, and spread this over the top of the pudding; return to the oven till a delicate brown.

ALMOND RICE PUDDING

Put one cupful each of well-washed rice and raisins into a pudding dish with six cupfuls of almond milk, one-third cup of sugar, and a pinch of salt. Bake in a moderate oven till tender, stirring up several times during the first ten minutes. Serve cold.

CORNSTARCH BLANC-MANGE

To one quart of milk add two tablespoonfuls of sugar, and heat just to boiling; then stir in five tablespoonfuls of cornstarch mixed thoroughly with two well-beaten eggs; flavor with lemon or vanilla, and pour into cups, previously wet in cold water, to mold. Place a mold of jelly in the center of a platter, and arrange the molds of blanc-mange around it. A portion of the blanc-mange may be colored and flavored with chocolate, so that each alternate mold on the platter will be brown. Serve with cream.

APPLE BATTER PUDDING

Pare and slice six medium-sized cooking apples into a buttered pudding dish, adding sugar to sweeten. Make a batter as follows: Beat three eggs to a foam; then add five tablespoonfuls of sifted flour, sprinkling it in while beating vigorously, and half a teaspoonful of salt. Stir in gradually enough milk to make of the consistency of thick cream, beat well, and pour over the apples, and bake until done. Serve with cream or rich milk.

APPLE TRIFLE

Pare, quarter, core, and stew six or eight apples to a pulp, adding the juice and grated rind of a lemon. When done, add sugar to sweeten, and turn into a deep glass dish. Heat a pint of milk to boiling, stir in three well-beaten eggs, saving out the white of one, and two tablespoonfuls of sugar, and cook until thickened. When cold pour over the apples in the dish. Beat the white of the egg to a stiff froth and drop by spoonfuls into a pan of boiling water for a moment, turn, then remove, and use to ornament the pudding.

APPLES WITH TAPIOCA

Soak a cupful of tapioca in two cupfuls of cold water for an hour; then spread on a clean white cloth, and place some pared and sliced apples, sugar, and grated lemon peel in the center; tie up the cloth loosely so that the tapioca will surround the apples, and put into boiling water; boil half an hour, or until done; then turn out the whole into a dish. Serve with boiled custard, whipped cream, or fruit jelly.

FRUIT TAPIOCA

Cook three-fourths cup of tapioca in four cups of water until smooth and transparent. Stir into it lightly a pint of fresh or canned strawberries, raspberries, or blackberries, adding sugar as required. Serve cold with cream, or a pint of fruit sauce.

PEACHES AND RICE

Soak a cup of rice in one and one-fourth cups of water for an hour; then add a cup of milk and a little salt, turn into a double boiler, cover, and steam for an hour, stirring occasionally for the first ten or fifteen minutes. When done, pour into a mold to cool, then turn out into a glass dish. Stew fresh or dried peaches in halves, and arrange them around the rice; pour the sirup or juice over the whole.

RICE WITH RAISINS

Wash and put to cook rice as directed above; after the rice has begun to swell, add a cupful of well-washed raisins. When done, serve with fruit juice, milk, or cream.

RICE WITH FIGS

Soak and cook the rice as directed for peaches and rice. Wash a small quantity of figs, and stew with a little sugar until thoroughly done; serve a spoonful of the figs with each dish of rice. The fig sauce should be so thick that it will not run over the rice.

APPLE RICE

Fill a pudding dish half full with tart apples, pared, quartered, cored, and sprinkled with sugar. Wash thoroughly half a cupful of rice and sprinkle over apples in pudding dish. Cover, steam until the rice is tender, and serve with cream and sugar.

APPLES WITH RAISINS

Pare, quarter, and core half a dozen good cooking apples. Wash a small cup of raisins, and put to cook in a quart of boiling water. When they have begun to swell, add the apples, a little sugar to sweeten, and cook until tender.

COCOANUT PUDDING

To one pint of milk, add two tablespoonfuls of desiccated cocoanut, and heat to boiling; remove the cocoanut by turning through a strainer; then add to the milk one-half cup of sugar and one-half cup of fine cracker or bread crumbs, cool a few minutes, then add the beaten yolks of two eggs. Turn into a pudding dish, set it inside a pan of hot water, and bake in the oven until set, but not watery. Beat the whites of the eggs to a stiff froth, add two teaspoonfuls of sugar, and spread on the top of the pudding; return to the oven to brown slightly.

CHERRY PUDDING

Soak a half cup of tapioca, and cook in a pint of water until transparent. Have ready in a pudding dish a pint of fresh, pitted cherries; sprinkle them with sugar, then pour over them the cooked tapioca, and bake for half an hour in a moderate oven. Serve with or without cream.

MINUTE PUDDING

Put one quart of milk into the inner vessel of a double boiler, or into an ordinary saucepan greased with a little butter, and heat to boiling; then stir in two small cups of flour, sifting it in a little at a time, and stirring briskly, that no lumps may be formed. Just before removing from the fire, add two well-beaten eggs, stir a moment, and serve at once with cream, and a little sugar if desired. If preferred, the eggs may be omitted.

ARROWROOT BLANC-MANGE

Heat a pint of milk to boiling; then stir in two heaping tablespoonfuls of arrowroot rubbed smooth in a half cup of cold milk, and a half cup of sugar; cook for a few minutes until thickened, stirring well, and pour into cups or molds previously wet in cold water, to cool. Serve with stewed fruit or fruit juice.

RICE SNOW WITH JELLY

Cook one cupful of rice in milk until tender, adding a little salt. When done, pile loosely in a dish; beat the whites of two or three eggs till stiff, mix with a half cupful of sugar, and pile in heaps like snow over the rice; ornament with bits of jelly, and, if in season, put a circle of fresh berries around the edge when ready to serve.

Simplicity is the highest art.

Many dishes have induced many diseases.—*Seneca.*

Study simplicity in the number of dishes, and variety in the character of the meals.

“It is not the chief end of man to gratify his appetite.”

CREAM MOLD

Heat two cups of milk to boiling; then add one-half cup of sugar, and three tablespoonfuls of ground rice, wet in a little cold milk; flavor with vanilla, and stir well until it thickens; pour into cups or molds previously wet in cold water, until set, then turn out on a large plate or into little dishes. Have ready a cup of whipped cream, and put some over each mold with a bit of jelly in the center of each, or serve with fruit sauce.

BOILED CUSTARD

Put one quart of milk and one-half cup of sugar into the inner vessel of a double boiler, let heat to boiling, then stir in slowly three eggs well beaten, and one tablespoonful of cornstarch rubbed smooth in a little cold milk; add any flavoring desired. Stir well, and when well set, turn into a dish to cool.

FLOATING ISLAND

Put a pint of milk into a double boiler; let heat to boiling, then add the well-beaten yolks of three eggs mixed with three tablespoonfuls of sugar. Stir well, and when done turn into the dish from which it is to be served. Beat the whites of the eggs to a stiff froth, and drop by spoonfuls for a few seconds into a pan of hot water; let them stand for a moment, then turn over, but do not allow them to harden. Remove with a skimmer or spoon, and put as islands on the top of the custard; let cool, then place bits of jelly on top of the islands.

APPLE FLOAT

To one pint of nice stewed apples, add the whites of three eggs beaten to a stiff froth, and four tablespoonfuls of white sugar; beat all together until very stiff. Have a glass dish filled with boiled custard made with two cups of milk, the yolks of the eggs, one teaspoonful of cornstarch, a tablespoonful of sugar, and flavoring if desired. Pile the apples on top, and serve.

BANANA CUSTARD

Slice six bananas into a deep dish. Heat one pint of milk to boiling; beat together one egg, one tablespoonful of sugar, and one dessertspoonful of cornstarch blended with a little milk, and stir into the hot milk; let boil up once or twice, then pour over the bananas, stirring them in.

ORANGE CUSTARD

Remove the peel from three large, sweet oranges, cut in halves, and rub through a colander. Heat one pint of milk to boiling, then add a tablespoonful of cornstarch dissolved in a little cold milk, and the beaten yolks of three eggs. When thickened, allow to cool, then stir in the oranges. Beat the whites of the eggs to a stiff froth, add two thirds of a cup of sugar, and spread on the top of the custard; place in the oven till slightly brown. Serve cold.

PINEAPPLE CUSTARD

Make a custard of one quart of milk, two thirds of a cup of sugar, and four eggs: heat the milk to boiling in a double boiler; then add the eggs and sugar beaten together. Stir well, and when done set aside to cool. Have a nice, ripe pineapple picked to pieces with a fork, and sprinkled with sugar. Just before serving the custard, stir in the pineapple.

TAPIOCA CREAM

Wash and soak four even tablespoonfuls of tapioca in a cup of water until soft; then add a little salt and a pint of milk, and heat to boiling in a double boiler; add the yolks of three eggs well beaten, and one-half cup of sugar; cook for a few minutes, then turn into an earthen dish; when cool, spread over the top the whites of the eggs beaten stiff with two tablespoonfuls of sugar, adding vanilla to flavor; place in the oven to brown slightly.

RICE CUSTARD

Wash one-half cup of rice, and cook in a double boiler in three cups of water or milk, or equal parts of each, until tender, adding a little salt; then add, while still on the range, one pint of milk, the yolks of three eggs well beaten, and five tablespoonfuls of sugar; stir gently, and cook only until thickened. Then turn into a pudding dish. Beat well the whites of three eggs, add three tablespoonfuls of powdered sugar, flavor with lemon or vanilla, and spread over the top of the custard; place in a slow oven to brown slightly.

Rich sauces and highly-seasoned dishes provoke thirst.—*Selected.*

Rich sauces are even worse than heaping several meats upon each other.—*Pliny.*

A wrong course of eating or drinking destroys health, and with it the sweetness of life. —*"Christian Temperance."*

SAUCES FOR VEGETABLES

TOMATO SAUCE

Cook one pint of fresh or canned tomatoes with a little onion, salt, and herb-flavor for fifteen minutes, then strain through a colander, and add two tablespoonfuls of flour browned with a tablespoonful of butter.

CREAM SAUCE

Melt two tablespoonfuls of butter in a saucepan over the fire, stir in two tablespoonfuls of flour, and cook about one minute, but do not let it brown. Add one cup of milk gradually, stirring constantly to keep smooth until thickened; cook very slowly, or steam over hot water, for ten minutes; add one-half teaspoonful of salt, and serve.

LENTIL SAUCE

Rub a cupful of cooked lentils through a colander into a saucepan; add a cup of milk and a little salt. When boiling, stir in a tablespoonful of browned flour rubbed smooth in a little cold milk. Add a little chopped parsley, if desired. For browned flour, see page 12.

BROWN SAUCE, NO. 1

Put a teaspoonful of butter into a frying-pan, and brown slightly; then pour in a pint of milk, and heat to boiling; stir in two tablespoonfuls of browned flour rubbed to a paste in a little cold water or milk; season with salt, boil until thickened, and serve.

BROWN SAUCE, NO. 2

Put a tablespoonful of butter into a frying-pan; when melted, sprinkle in two tablespoonfuls of flour, stirring until nicely browned; then add enough boiling water to make of the consistency of cream, stirring constantly to prevent lumps from forming. Add salt to taste.

PARSLEY SAUCE

Make a brown sauce, and add a little finely chopped parsley just before serving.

EGG AND MILK SAUCE

To a pint of milk add a tablespoonful or two of cream, or a teaspoonful of butter, and heat to boiling; then stir in one even tablespoonful of flour rubbed smooth in a little cold water or milk; let boil a few minutes, stirring constantly; then stir in rapidly the well-beaten yolk of one egg; season with salt, boil up, and serve.

BREAD SAUCE

Put a tablespoonful of oil and a teaspoonful of grated onion into a saucepan, and allow to heat, but not scorch; then add a cupful of rich milk, or nut milk, and a little salt. When heated nearly to boiling, stir in one-half cupful of sifted bread crumbs. Let boil slowly a few minutes, and serve. Nice with protose cutlets or baked potatoes.

MINT SAUCE

Take fresh, green mint, wash, and chop very fine. Put into a glass, and for each two tablespoonfuls of mint allow one tablespoonful of sugar, and the juice of one lemon diluted with an equal amount of water.

SAUCES FOR DESSERTS

ARROWROOT SAUCE

Heat one cup of water to boiling; then add one teaspoonful of sugar, and one small tablespoonful of arrowroot mixed smooth in a little cold water, stirring briskly. In a few minutes remove from the fire, and flavor with lemon or almond. Nice for puddings.

BOILED CUSTARD SAUCE

Beat together in a saucepan, two eggs, one tablespoonful of sugar, and one-half teaspoonful of cornstarch. Place over the fire one cupful of milk, and as soon as it begins to boil pour it over the eggs in the saucepan. Stir well, place over the fire to boil until it thickens, then pour into a pitcher, and flavor if desired.

CHOCOLATE SAUCE

Mix two tablespoonfuls of shaved chocolate with two cupfuls of sweet milk, and heat to boiling; then add the well-beaten yolks of two eggs, stirring briskly; boil a few minutes until thickened, and remove from the fire; add the whites of the eggs, which have been beaten to a stiff froth, and two tablespoonfuls of white sugar. Nice with cornstarch blanc-mange.

ORANGE SAUCE

Heat a pint of water to boiling, and thicken with a tablespoonful of cornstarch; add a cupful of orange juice extracted from good sweet oranges, a small piece of the yellow rind for flavoring, and sugar to sweeten; the beaten yolk of an egg may be added if desired; remove the orange rind before serving.

LEMON SAUCE

To a pint of boiling water add a slice or two of lemon, and thicken with a small tablespoonful of cornstarch; remove the lemon, cook a few minutes until clear, then add two thirds of a cup of sugar, the juice of one lemon, and a beaten egg if desired; boil up, cool, and serve.

FRUIT SAUCE

Obtain the juice of raspberries, strawberries, grapes, currants, or any larger fruit, by simmering for a short time with a little water, and straining through a thin cloth; heat the juice to scalding, then slightly thicken with cornstarch rubbed smooth in a little cold water, allowing a tablespoonful of cornstarch for each pint of juice; cook a few minutes till thickened, and sweeten to taste. Three or four tablespoonfuls of fruit jelly dissolved in a pint of hot water makes a good substitute for fruit juice if the latter is not available.

STRAWBERRY SAUCE

Beat one and one-half cups of powdered sugar and one tablespoonful of butter to a cream. Then add the stiffly beaten white of one egg and beat till very light. Set in a cool place, and when ready to serve, add one pint of mashed strawberries.

WHIPPED CREAM

Beat one cup of cold sweet cream with a Dover egg-beater until stiff; then beat in two tablespoonfuls of powdered sugar, and one-half teaspoonful extract of vanilla; set in a cool place till ready to serve. Have the cream cold, and not too thick, or it will turn to butter while beating. A nice sauce for desserts.

"To keep in health this rule is wise,
Eat only when you need and relish food,
Chew thoroughly, that it may do you good,
Have it well cooked, unspiced, and undisguised."

Food for repentance—mince pie eaten late at night.

He who eats till he is sick must fast till he is well.—*Selected.*

How many homes are cursed by discomfort and ill health, and thoughts and bitter words, simply because the wife does not know how to cook.—*The Young Woman.*

One of the greatest objections to pies is that they are generally made too rich. When a large amount of grease is employed in making the crust, and the filling is seasoned heavily with spices and various condiments, they can hardly fail to be unwholesome.

But pies need not be made in this way. If proper ingredients are used, and simplicity is studied in making them, there is no reason why they should be seriously objectionable.

Pie Dish

There are two styles of pie in general use,—one, the English style, baked in a deep dish, frequently with only a top crust; the other, the American, baked in a shallow dish, usually with two crusts, an upper and an under. Custard, cream, lemon, and pumpkin pies, however, have only an under crust. Most of the recipes here given are for the shallow pies with two crusts.

Custard, pumpkin, and other pies in which milk and eggs are used, should be baked in a slow oven. They will also be improved if the milk used be hot. To stir beaten eggs into the hot milk, add a few spoonfuls of cold milk to the eggs, then pour into the hot milk, a little at a time, stirring well.

The filling for pies should always be prepared before making the crust, unless the crust is to be baked first. All the material should be cold, except for custard and pumpkin pies, and should be put together quickly, handling as little as possible, and without kneading the dough.

Rolling-pin

When the paste is ready, take sufficient for one crust, and roll out on a floured board quickly and lightly until about an eighth of an inch in thickness, and a little larger than the pie dish, as it will shrink when lifted from the board. When rolled thin, flour or oil the pie dish, cover smoothly with the crust, and fill, adding sugar as required. Sprinkle a little flour over the sugar; this thickens the juice slightly, and prevents the upper crust from becoming soggy. For custard or fruit pies with wet fillings, brush the bottom crust with the white of an egg before putting in the filling. The crust will then remain dry and tender.

Pie

If there is to be a top crust, roll it out in the same manner, and make a few ornamental cuts in the center to allow the steam to escape. Wet the edge of the lower crust, and lift on the upper crust, pressing the edges together so that the juice may not escape. Trim away the overhanging portions, and with the thumb and fingers press the edge into a scalloped or ornamental wall, as shown in the accompanying cut. Especially should this be done when only an under crust is used, that the pie may be handled with greater ease. It also adds to the appearance of the pie. Pies are generally better eaten the same day they are baked.

PLAIN PIE CRUST

For each pie with two crusts take two small cups of sifted flour, and work thoroughly into it three tablespoonfuls of butter, adding a little salt; wet with just sufficient cold water to make a rather stiff dough; mix quickly, roll out thin, and bake as soon as the pie can be made. A good crust may be made with olive-oil, or fresh cocoanut or vegetable oil, instead of butter, using about the same quantity.

CREAM PIE CRUST

Take two scant cups of fine, sifted flour, or equal parts of fine flour and Graham flour, add a little salt, and moisten with enough cold, thin sweet cream to make a rather stiff dough; roll out thin, place in the pie dish, fill, and bake quickly.

APPLE PIE

Pare, core, and slice thin, tart ripe apples; line the pie dish with a crust, and fill with the apples; sprinkle with sugar, and add two or three tablespoonfuls of cold water. Cover with an upper crust, according to general directions, and bake until a light brown. Apples that do not cook quickly may be stewed until about half done before making into pies. Apple pie when cold is very nice served with sweet cream.

PEACH PIE

Pare, remove stones, and make the same as apple pie.

GOOSEBERRY PIE

Remove the stems and blossom ends, wash, and fill a pie dish lined with a crust. Add a half cup of sugar, and sprinkle with flour. Prepare the upper crust, cover, and bake. To prevent the juice from running out while baking, make a paste of a teaspoonful of flour and a little water, and brush over the edge of the under crust before putting on the top crust. If desired, beat together the white of an egg and a tablespoonful of fine sugar, and meringue the top of the pie when done; return to the oven, and brown slightly.

RHUBARB PIE

Wash, strip off the skin, and cut the stalks into thin slices. Line a pie dish with crust, and fill with the rhubarb. Add a half cup of sugar, two or three tablespoonfuls of water, and sprinkle over a tablespoonful of flour. Wet the edges of the lower crust, place on a prepared top crust, press the edges together, trim, and bake. Equal portions of rhubarb and apples may be used in the place of all rhubarb.

RASPBERRY PIE

Look over the raspberries, line a pie dish with a crust and fill with berries; add two tablespoonfuls of sugar, a little water, sprinkle with flour, and proceed as with gooseberry pie.

BLACKBERRY PIE

Look over about one pint of blackberries, and proceed the same as for raspberry pie. Blueberry pie may be made in the same way.

CHERRY PIE

Take nice ripe cherries, remove the stones if preferred, and make the same as raspberry pie, adding sugar according to the acidity of the fruit.

DRIED CURRANT PIE

Wash the currants in two or three waters through a colander to remove sand and grit, and stew; when cool, line a pie dish with crust, and fill with the currants, pouring in a small quantity of the juice; add a little sugar, then sprinkle over with two tablespoonfuls of flour, cover with a crust, and bake in a hot oven till done. It should not be made too dry.

PRUNE PIE

Wash the prunes well in warm water, rinse, soak, and put to cook without draining, cover, and stew slowly from one to two hours. When done, put through a colander to remove stones and skins. Bake with two crusts. Very little sugar will be needed. If the pulp is quite juicy, a tablespoonful of flour may be sprinkled over.

LEMON PIE

To one cupful of boiling water, add one heaping tablespoonful of cornstarch blended with a little cold water. Boil up, remove from the fire, and stir in two-thirds cup of sugar; let cool, then add the beaten yolks of two eggs, and the juice and grated rind of a lemon. Bake with under crust only; when done, meringue the top with a tablespoonful of sugar and the whites of the eggs beaten stiff; return to a slow oven to brown slightly.

DRIED APPLE PIE

Take good dried apples, wash, and soak for several hours, or overnight, in sufficient cold water to cover them. Stew, without draining, until soft; mash fine, adding lemon flavoring and sugar to sweeten; bake with two crusts, or ornament with strips or lattice-work crust on top. A few stewed blackberries or raspberries may be added to the apples.

DRIED PEACH PIE

Stew until soft, mash to a pulp, add sugar to sweeten, and make the same as dried apple pie. If desired, one-third apricots may be used.

RAISIN PIE

For three pies, stew one pound of raisins for nearly an hour in enough water to cover them; add the juice of a lemon, and a small cup of white sugar. Line the pie dishes with crust, fill with raisins and a little of the juice, and sprinkle two tablespoonfuls of flour over each pie. Bake with two crusts. For lemon raisin pie add the juice and grated rind of one lemon.

CREAM PIE

Put one cup of milk to scald in a double boiler. Beat together two eggs, leaving out the white of one, two even teaspoonfuls of sifted flour stirred smooth in a little cold milk, and two heaping tablespoonfuls of sugar. When the milk is scalding hot, add this mixture, and stir for a minute or two until it thickens. It is better not to cook after it is thick, and the less it is stirred, except to keep it from forming into lumps, the better; add vanilla or lemon to flavor. Line the pie dish with a crust, pricking well with a fork to prevent blistering, and bake in a quick oven; then put the cream, which is already sufficiently cooked, into the baked crust. Beat the white of the egg to a stiff froth with a tablespoonful of sugar, and spread on top of the pie. Place in the oven to brown slightly.

CUSTARD PIE

Line a pie dish with a crust, and fill with the following: Three eggs, three tablespoonfuls of sugar, and one teaspoonful of flour; beat thoroughly together, and add milk enough to fill the dish. Bake slowly until set, but do not allow to boil. As soon as it puffs, and a knife can be cut into the custard and come out clean, it is done. To be eaten cold, and on the same day as baked.

PUMPKIN PIE

Cut the pumpkin in halves, remove the seeds, cut in slices, and stew until dry and soft. Mash smooth, and for each pie take one cup of stewed pumpkin, one-third cup of sugar, two eggs, and about a pint of milk. Beat the eggs and sugar together, stir in the pumpkin, and, lastly, add the milk; mix well, and bake with an under crust only, until the custard is set. Squash may be used instead of pumpkin. If more convenient, two tablespoonfuls of flour may be used in place of the eggs. A tablespoonful or two of molasses may also be added if desired.

What moistens the lip, and
   What brightens the eye,
What brings back the past,
   Like a good pumpkin pie?—*Whittier.*

PIE WITH UPPER CRUST ONLY

Take a deep pie dish, place a small cup upside down in the middle of it, and fill the dish with fruit, adding sugar as desired. Place a border of crust around the edge of the dish, put on the top crust, ornament the edges, and bake.

TARTS

Line shallow pie dishes or patty-pans with good crusts, fill with the fruit, and bake. When done, remove from the oven, and sprinkle with fine sugar.

Small tarts may be made by rolling crust out thin, and cutting in shapes with a cake cutter, using half of them for the under crust, and the other half for tops; ornament the tops by cutting small holes in the center with a thimble or small fancy mold. Bake quickly, and when done put together with fruit jelly.

VEGETABLE PIE

Boil for a short time several potatoes and onions, after which slice them into a deep, buttered pie dish in layers; add to each layer a little sage and well-steeped tapioca, and season with salt. Cover with a crust and bake. A very economical and wholesome pie.

SAVORY PIE

Soak one-half cup of tapioca in one cup of cold water for one hour. Moisten enough stale bread in cold water to make three cupfuls; put into a dish, and rub in two tablespoonfuls of butter and one of flour. Then mix in one-half cup of stewed fresh or canned tomatoes, two beaten eggs, one small onion chopped fine, one tablespoonful of powdered sage, and salt to taste. Put into a buttered pudding dish and pour over the tapioca. Boil two eggs until hard, remove shells, cut into slices, and place on top of the tapioca; add a few bits of butter, cover with a crust, and bake in a moderate oven for twenty or thirty minutes. Serve hot.

MERINGUE FOR PIES

To each stiffly beaten white of an egg, add a tablespoonful of sugar, and spread on the pie after it is baked and allowed to cool slightly; place in the oven for a few minutes. Care should be taken that the oven is not too hot, or the covering will be tough and leathery.

Feed sparingly, and defy the physician.
Who lives to eat, will die by eating.

Whoever eats too much, or of food which is not healthful, is weakening his powers to resist the clamors of other appetites and passions.—"*Christian Temperance.*"

The best seasoning for food is hunger.—*Socrates.*

Reason should direct, and appetite obey.—*Cicero.*

Men should be temperate in eating as well as drinking.—*Dr. Brandreth.*

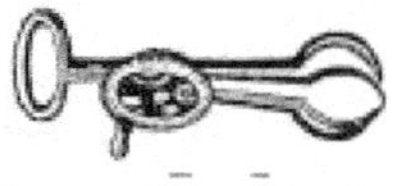

Dover Egg Beater

It is important that all the necessary materials should be gathered together before beginning the cake. If baking-powder is used, allow a teaspoonful to each cup of flour; sift it in the flour, and measure the sugar; have the pans for baking in readiness. Beat the whites and yolks of eggs separately in china bowls, using a Dover egg-beater. The whites should be beaten till stiff enough to cut with a knife, the yolks till they cease to froth and begin to thicken. Cream the butter by beating it, first warming the dish by rinsing with hot water, if the weather is cold. Then add the sugar slowly, then the beaten yolks of eggs; add a little of the milk, then a part of the flour, thus alternating with the milk and flour till all are used, being careful to have the mixture always of about the same consistency.

Next fold in the stiffly beaten whites, add flavoring if desired, and beat for a few moments. If fruit is used, fold it in, well floured, the last thing, or it will sink to the bottom of the cake.

The baking is an important part of cake-making. The oven should be at a proper temperature; if too hot at first, the cake browns too quickly, and a crust is formed over the top before the cake has sufficient time to rise; if not hot enough, the air that has been beaten in escapes before the heat has time to expand it; the result is that the cake is coarse-grained and heavy.

Have the oven less hot for cake than for bread, but hotter for thin cake than for loaf cake. It is about right for loaf cake made with butter when it turns a piece of writing-paper a light brown in five minutes. About an hour will be required to bake a loaf cake: from fifteen to twenty minutes for small cakes and layer cakes.

Cake Pan

A tube cake pan, as shown in the accompanying cut, is very good for baking ordinary cakes, as the tube causes the cake to bake more evenly, and renders it less liable to fall.

If it is necessary to move the cake after putting it in the oven, it should be done carefully, as jarring is liable to make it fall. A cake is done when a clean broom straw passed through the thickest part comes out clean.

If a cake rises up, cracks open, and remains that way, it has baked too fast, or too much flour has been used. To bake properly, it should rise first on the edges, then in the middle, crack open slightly, then settle till level, when it will have closed nearly together again. The outside should be a golden brown, the inside slightly moist, and fine grained.

In beating the yolks of eggs where both eggs and milk are used, first rinse the bowl in which the yolks are to be beaten with a little of the milk.

In beating the whites of the eggs, do not stop until they are stiff, as they can not be beaten stiff after standing till they have become liquid again. Eggs will beat stiffer if cold, and beaten in a cold dish and in a cool room.

Jelly for filling should be beaten till smooth, then spread between the layers before they are quite cool. In using dessicated cocoanut, first moisten it with a little sweet cream.

Citron used in cake should be cut into fine strips. Currants and raisins should be looked over, washed, dried, and then be well floured before being added to the cake, as they absorb moisture and tend to make the cake heavy. Rich cake should be avoided. Sponge cake may be considered the most healthful.

To make sponge cake, beat the yolks till thick and light-colored, then beat in the sugar, add lemon-juice, or other liquid and flavoring to be used. Then add the stiffly beaten whites, sift in the flour over them, and fold all in together without stirring or beating. Beating sponge cake after adding the flour makes it firm and tough, as also does the addition of too much flour. Sponge cake should be put together lightly and quickly, and baked at once.

SPONGE CAKE

Beat the yolks of three eggs; then gradually add one cupful of granulated sugar, one tablespoonful each of cold water and lemon-juice. Add the beaten whites and one cupful of flour, following general directions for making sponge cake as given above.

LEMON SPONGE CAKE

Take four eggs, one cup of sugar, one tablespoonful of lemon-juice, with a little of the grated rind, and one cupful of flour. Beat the yolks of the eggs to a foam, then beat in the sugar, adding a little at a time; then add the lemon-juice and grated rind; beat the whites of the eggs until very stiff, then lightly fold and chop them into the mixture. Slowly sift in the flour, carefully working it in. Do not beat after the flour has been added. Bake in two layers, and put together with fruit jelly or lemon honey. See page 40.

SPONGE LOAF CAKE

Break ten eggs into a large bowl, add two large cupfuls of granulated sugar, and beat together for half an hour without pausing. Then add one cupful of sifted flour, the juice and grated rind of one lemon, and one-fourth cup of cold water. Turn into deep pans, sprinkle the top lightly with powdered sugar, and bake about an hour in a moderate oven.

GEM CAKES

Beat to a foam the yolk of one egg, one cup of sugar, and one cup of cold, thin, sweet cream; a little grated lemon rind may be added for flavoring. Stir in slowly, beating thoroughly, two cupfuls of flour into which a heaping tablespoonful of cornstarch has been sifted. Beat until light and smooth; then add the well-beaten whites of two eggs, stirring just enough to mix them in. Turn into oiled, heated gem irons, and bake in a rather quick oven.

RICE CAKES

Separate four eggs; add a pinch of salt to the whites, beat until stiff, then set in a cool place. Beat the yolks for several minutes, then slowly add one cupful of sugar, beating continuously; carefully fold in the beaten whites, and lastly add one-half cup of flour, sifted before measuring, and mixed with one-half cup of ground rice; work in carefully, and quickly turn the mixture into oiled patty-pans, or drop by spoonfuls into a large oiled baking pan, and bake in a quick oven.

CREAM CAKE

One cupful each of sugar and sweet milk, one egg, one tablespoonful of butter, two cupfuls of flour, and two teaspoonfuls of baking-powder. Put together according to general directions. Bake in three layers, and put together with a filling made as follows: Heat one cupful of milk to boiling; to this add one-fourth cup of sugar, one dessertspoonful of flour rubbed smooth in a little cold milk reserved for this purpose, and one well-beaten egg; boil until thickened, let cool a little, and spread between the layers.

NUT CAKE

One and one-half cups of sugar, two tablespoonfuls of butter, two eggs, two cupfuls of flour, with two teaspoonfuls of baking-powder, and one cupful of milk. Put together according to general directions. Lastly, stir in one cupful of chopped nuts, and bake in a moderate oven.

FAVORITE CAKE

Beat together for nearly an hour one cupful each of flour and rice flour, twelve eggs, two cupfuls of sugar, and a spoonful of caraway seeds. Bake in a tube cake pan.

LAYER CAKE

One and one-half cups sugar, half cup of butter, three eggs, half cup of milk, and two heaping cups of sifted flour, with two teaspoonfuls of baking powder. Bake in three layers, and put together with a boiled frosting to which a cupful of chopped nuts or raisins may be added.

DELICATE CUP CAKE

Take two eggs, beaten separately, one cup of sugar, one cup of rich milk, two cups of flour, and teaspoonful of vanilla. Make according to general directions; bake in patty pans, or gem irons.

RAISED FRUIT CAKE

Take one cup of light bread dough when ready for the pans, put into a dish, and work into it one-half cup of oil or butter, one egg well beaten, one cup of sugar, one-half cup of milk, one and one-half cups of flour, and lastly one cup of English currants or seedless raisins, chopped fine. Turn into an oiled bread tin, let rise in a warm place for about an hour and a half, or until light, then bake for nearly an hour in a moderate oven.

FROSTING FOR CAKE

Beat the white of one egg until stiff, add a teaspoonful of lemon-juice, then gradually add one scant cup of powdered sugar; beat very hard; flavor as desired. To color it a delicate pink, add a little currant or strawberry juice; a yellow tint may be obtained by grating orange or lemon rind, and using two tablespoonfuls of the juice, first straining through a cloth.

BOILED FROSTING

Without stirring boil one cupful of sugar and two tablespoonfuls of water in a saucepan until clear; then pour it upon the stiffly beaten white of an egg, stirring well together, and spread over the cake with a knife, which dip frequently into cold water.

CREAM ICING

To two tablespoonfuls of cream and one teaspoonful of vanilla or other flavoring add enough confectioner's sugar to make it stiff enough to spread. Orange, or other fruit juice, may be used in place of the cream.

ORANGE ICING

Beat the yolk of one egg and add the juice and grated rind of one orange and enough confectioner's sugar to make it stiff enough to spread.

Write it underneath your feet,
Up and down the busy street;
Write it for the great and small,
In the palace, cottage, hall,—
Where there's drink there's danger.
—*Selected.*

Water is best.—*Pindar.*

Tea is a stimulant; coffee is a hurtful indulgence.

Wine is a mocker, strong drink is raging; and whosoever is deceived thereby is not wise.—*Solomon.*

If you wish to keep mind clear and body healthy, abstain from all fermented liquors.—*Sydney Smith.*

Many who never touch alcohol ruin their health by tea.—*Hygiene Review.*

Temperance is the parent of health, cheerfulness, and old age.—*George Mogridge.*

CEREAL COFFEE

Coffee Strainer

To prepare, take three and one-half quarts of fresh bran, one and one-half quarts corn-meal, two cupfuls of molasses, and one cupful of boiling water; mix all together thoroughly, bake in a large dripping-pan in the oven till a rich brown color; stir often to prevent scorching. Make the same as ordinary coffee, only let boil a little longer.

CRUST COFFEE

Brown stale pieces of brown or white bread in the oven slowly to a golden brown; then crush with a rolling-pin. Put the crumbs in a thin cloth bag, filling only half full, and tying near the top; put the bag in the coffee-pot and turn on hot water, allowing seven parts of water to one of crumbs. Boil five or ten minutes. Remove the bag, bring the coffee to a boil again, and serve with cream and sugar. This makes a very smooth drink, and is especially nice for the sick.

CORN COFFEE

Coffee Mill

Brown common field corn as brown as possible without burning; then pound, or grind coarsely in a coffee-mill, and place in a covered can ready for use. In making the coffee, mix the white of an egg with three tablespoonfuls of the ground grain, pour over three or four cups of boiling water, and steep for ten or fifteen minutes. Serve with cream and sugar.

Peas, wheat, barley, or rice may be prepared in the same way.

HOT MILK

Heat the milk in a double boiler until the surface becomes wrinkled. It should be drunk a few sips at a time. A bowl of hot milk and brown bread forms a nourishing meal.

CAMBRIC TEA

Take a cup of boiling water, add a little cream, and sugar to sweeten. A simple but pleasant and wholesome drink.

EGG-NOG

Beat one egg and a teaspoonful of powdered sugar to a foam; add the juice of half a lemon, pour into a glass and fill up with cold water.

EGG-NOG, HOT

Beat well together the yolk of one egg and a tablespoonful of sugar; add one-half cup of hot milk or water, and the white of the egg beaten to a stiff froth; stir lightly, and serve.

LEMONADE, NO. 1

Roll the lemons till soft; cut into halves, and with a lemon drill squeeze out sufficient juice to make one cupful; add to this one cupful of white sugar; as soon as the sugar dissolves, add about two quarts of water, and serve. For lemon frappé add the beaten whites of three eggs.

Lemon Drill

LEMONADE, NO. 2

For each quart desired, take the juice of three or four lemons, and the rind of one. Peel the rind very thin, getting just the yellow; place it in a pitcher with the juice of the lemons and from four to six tablespoonfuls of white sugar. Pour over enough hot water to make a quart in all; cover at once, and let stand until cold; or pour over a spoonful or two of boiling water to dissolve the sugar, and add the necessary quantity of cold water.

HOT LEMONADE

To the juice of each lemon add a cupful of boiling water, and sweeten to taste. Excellent for a cold.

ORANGEADE

Choose nice, juicy, ripe oranges, and make the same as Lemonade Nos. 1 and 2, only using less sugar. This will be found a much nicer drink than many imagine. Try it.

FRUIT JUICE LEMONADE

To a pint of lemonade prepared according to foregoing recipes, add a half cup of strawberry, raspberry, blackberry, or currant juice. This gives a nice color to the lemonade, besides improving its flavor.

PINEAPPLE LEMONADE

Make the lemonade as indicated above, and flavor with a few spoonfuls of pineapple juice.

GRAPEADE

Take two pounds of thoroughly ripe purple grapes, crush, and strain the juice through a coarse cloth or jelly-bag. Add to the juice three tablespoonfuls of white sugar, and dilute with sufficient cold water to suit the taste.

FRUIT JUICE DRINKS

Take a small quantity of the juice of any stewed or canned fruit. Dilute with water, and add sugar according to the acidity of the juice. When fruit juice is not available, similar drinks may be made by dissolving fruit jelly in warm water, and allowing to cool. Such drinks are especially refreshing for the sick.

FRUIT PUNCH

Boil two pounds of sugar and three quarts of water for five minutes. Then strain, and add to it the juice of two lemons and two oranges, and one pint of freshly grated pineapple. Let stand for an hour or two, then add sufficient shaved ice to make it palatable, a cupful of halved strawberries, a few raspberries, and serve.

BUTTERMILK

If rich and thick, drop into it a piece of ice; or if not, place on ice till cool. This is a very healthful drink, for, after the butter, which is the carbonaceous or heat-producing element, is removed, a most refreshing, nourishing quality remains.

Nuts, Oils, Etc.

O blessed health! thou art above all gold and treasure. He who has thee has little more to wish for; and he who is so wretched as to want thee, wants everything with thee.—*Sterne.*

Give a wise man health, and he will give himself every other thing.—*Colton.*

It is health that makes your meat savory, your drink palatable, your sleep refreshing, your delights delightful, and your pleasures pleasurable.—*Combe.*

THE world is in need of knowledge how to prepare and use simple, inexpensive, healthful foods. As diseases increase in the animal creation, it will be more and more necessary for those who desire to preserve their health to come back to the diet originally given to man,—a diet consisting chiefly of fruits, grains, and nuts, and various legumes, roots, and herbs. At the rate disease is increasing at the present time, it will not be long before it will be unsafe to use animal products of any kind. It is well, therefore, for all to learn how to prepare foods without them.

Various nut, cereal, and legume preparations well supply the place of flesh-meats. The different nut and vegetable oils take the place of butter, cream, and other animal fats.

In the use of nuts, care should be taken not to use them too freely, as they are a very rich and concentrated form of food. Eaten sparingly in their natural state in connection with the meals, or properly combined with other less concentrated foods, they fill an important place in a natural dietary.

A little experience in the use of vegetable oils will convince any one that they are not only palatable, but far more cleanly and wholesome than many of the ordinary fats used in cooking.

The following recipes are designed to aid especially in preparing foods in this manner:—

PEANUT BUTTER

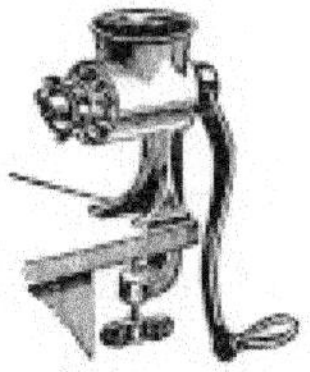

Universal Chopper and Nut-Butter Mill

Put the shelled peanuts in a pan in a slow oven, leaving the door slightly ajar; allow to stay in till so dry that the hulls will rub off easily, but in no case allow to brown or burn. When sufficiently dry, put into a bag, tie up closely, and knead or roll on a table with the hands until the husks are well loosened; separate the husks from the nuts by turning from one pan into another in the wind. Grind, and cook for several hours in a double boiler with no water added to the nuts. Put away to use as occasion requires.

PEANUT CREAM

Mix one tablespoonful of nut butter with two or three spoonfuls of water to a smooth cream; then add one-half cupful of water, a little salt, and stir well together.

PEANUT MILK

Make the same as peanut cream, only add more water.

ALMOND BUTTER

Pour boiling water over the shelled nuts, and let stand from three to five minutes; then drain, and slip off the husks with thumb and finger. Put in a warm place till thoroughly dry; grind, and put away for future use.

ALMOND MILK AND CREAM

Proceed the same as with peanut cream and milk, only using a little more water.

COCOANUT MILK AND CREAM

Cocoanut Scraper

Select good cocoanuts with milk in them. Let the milk out of the soft eye; then, holding the nut in the left hand, strike sharp, quick blows with a hammer or iron bar on the meridian line, causing the nut to revolve by tossing it up slightly, when it will break in halves. Grate on an iron or steel cocoanut scraper, made as shown in accompanying cut, placing the scraper board across a chair, with a pan upon the floor to catch the grated nut, while the operator sits upon the board, takes half of the broken nut in the hollow of both hands, scraping it back and forth over the sharp teeth till all the meat has been finely scraped from the shell. For each grated nut pour over a quart of hot water; stir well, then squeeze and strain through a strong, coarse cloth. Empty the cocoanut from the cloth into a saucepan, pour over a little more hot water, stir, and strain through the cloth a second time, to get out all the milk. This makes cocoanut milk. Using half the quantity of water makes good cream; or let the milk stand an hour and skim off the top for thick cream.

COCOANUT-OIL

Cocoanut-oil can generally be purchased in the market from wholesale druggists, though it is sometimes difficult to get that which is not rancid. It can be made by taking the cream from a half dozen or dozen nuts, treated as above, only allowing the milk to stand over night before skimming, and boiling the cream in an iron vessel, without stirring, until all the water is evaporated. When done, the sediment will be found browned, and adhering to the bottom of the vessel. Bottle, and set away for use.

Ko-nut is a pure, refined cocoanut-oil, which does not turn rancid, and is, therefore, very nice, and far preferable to the cocoanut-oil ordinarily obtainable for cooking purposes.

VEGETABLE OIL

There are various good cooking oils, among which may be mentioned Wesson's Cooking Oil, and Fairbank's White Cooking Oil, both refined products of cottonseed-oil. Olive-oil may also be used in cooking.

HOME-MADE GRANOLA

Take slices of brown, white, or whole wheat bread, place in a moderate oven until a light brown, break in pieces, and grind coarsely through a mill. Or, take a cup each of wheat-meal and white flour, one-half cup each of corn-meal and rolled oats or corn-meal and rye flour, and enough cold water to make a stiff dough; knead well, roll thin, cut in squares, and bake until dry and brittle; grind coarsely, and serve with thin cream, hot or cold milk, cocoanut milk, or fruit juice; or to each pint of boiling milk or water stir in one cupful of granola, add a little salt, cook a few minutes, and serve.

NUTMEAT

Take one cup of peanut butter, one and one-half cups hot water, three heaping tablespoonfuls of gluten, and one level teaspoonful of salt. Mix all well together, and cook in a double boiler from four to five hours. A small onion grated fine and a teaspoonful of powdered sage may be added if desired.

PROTOSE STEAK

Cut protose into slices half an inch thick. Lay on an oiled tin and place in the oven until nicely browned.

PROTOSE CUTLETS

Take one pound of protose and cut into slices three or four inches long and one inch wide, lay on an oiled tin, and place in the oven till well heated; have ready an egg well beaten, to which add a sprinkle of salt; take the protose from the oven, and dip each piece in the beaten egg, then roll in fine bread crumbs, place back on the pan, and set in the oven until nicely browned.

NUT GRAVY

Blend one tablespoonful of nut butter with a little water; stir it into a pint of boiling water; salt, and thicken with two tablespoonfuls of browned flour moistened with cold water; boil five or ten minutes. A few spoonfuls of stewed, strained tomatoes will improve it. Nice with vegetables or toasts.

EGGS IN NEST ON ZWIEBACK

Take six eggs, or as many as required, break, and separate, by putting all the whites in one bowl and each yolk in a cup by itself containing a spoonful or two of cold water. Moisten six slices of zwieback by pouring over them hot water and quickly draining, and place side by side in a large shallow baking pan. Beat the whites of the eggs until very stiff, and place an equal amount on top of each slice of zwieback. Make a hollow in the center of the whites, lift the yolks out of the water from the cups with a tablespoon, being careful not to break them, and place a yolk in each hollow. Sprinkle over a little salt, and place in the oven until the whites are a delicate brown. Serve as soon as done. A nice dish for the sick.

Health—thou chiefest good,
  Bestow'd by heaven,
But seldom understood.
—*Lucan.*

Diet cures more than doctors.—*Scotch Proverb.*

A merry heart doeth good like a medicine.—*Solomon.*

Health is not quoted in the markets, because it is without price.—*Selected.*

The best physicians are Dr. Diet, Dr. Quiet, and Dr. Merryman.—*Selected.*

The less the attention is called to the stomach the better. If you are in constant fear that your food will hurt you, it most assuredly will. Forget your troubles; think of something cheerful.—"*Christian Temperance.*"

FOOD for the sick should generally be of a very simple character. It should be such as will furnish the most nourishment with the least tax upon the digestive organs. It should be prepared with care and scrupulous cleanliness, well cooked, and served in the most inviting manner. Cover the tray with clean white linen, and use the daintiest dishes the house affords.

Other dishes suitable for the sick may be found among the Toasts, Breads, Fruits, Wholesome Drinks, etc.

GLUTEN GRUEL

For each cupful of boiling milk stir in one tablespoonful of gluten meal; add a little salt, let boil a moment, and serve.

ARROWROOT GRUEL

Rub one teaspoonful of arrowroot smooth in a tablespoonful of cold water; pour over it two cups of boiling water, stirring continually; set the saucepan in hot water till the arrowroot is thoroughly cooked; turn into a pitcher, add a little sugar to sweeten, and flavor with a little lemon peel.

GRAHAM GRUEL

Into three cups of actively boiling water, stir one small cup of sifted Graham flour mixed to a paste with a cup of cold water or milk. Add a little salt, and cook until done. Add a small quantity of cream or rich milk, and serve. An excellent breakfast dish for well people also, especially for children.

CREAMED GRUEL

Cook one tablespoonful of rolled oats in a scant pint of water until tender; then strain through a sieve. Add one-half cup of thin cream, and salt to taste; let just come to a boil, remove from the fire, then stir in the whites of two eggs beaten to a stiff froth. Add a little sugar if desired.

RICE GRUEL

Wet one teaspoonful of rice flour in a little cold milk, and stir into one pint of boiling water; salt slightly, and boil until transparent. Flavor with lemon peel.

MILK GRUEL

Heat one cup of milk to boiling, and stir in one tablespoonful of fine oatmeal; add a cup of boiling water, and cook until the meal is thoroughly done. Season with a little salt.

ONION GRUEL

Boil a few sliced onions until tender in a pint of fresh milk, adding a little oatmeal; season with salt. Good for colds.

LEMONADE, HOT AND COLD

Make as indicated on page 92.

APPLE WATER

Take three ripe, tart, juicy apples, wash and wipe, but do not pare; slice into a quart of hot water; let stand until cool, pour off the water, and sweeten it to taste.

RICE WATER

Put into a saucepan one-half cup of well-washed rice; add three cups of cold water, and boil for thirty minutes. Strain, season with salt, and serve.

BARLEY WATER

Put two tablespoonfuls of pearl barley into a cupful of boiling water, and let simmer a few minutes; drain, and add two quarts of boiling water with a few figs and seeded raisins chopped fine. Cook slowly until reduced one-half; strain; add sugar to taste, and a little of the juice and rind of a lemon if desired.

BAKED APPLE

Bake a nice, tart apple, as directed on page 37; serve with cream, or, when done, cover with a meringue made of the beaten white of an egg and a teaspoonful of powdered sugar, and lightly brown in the oven.

CUP CUSTARD

To one well-beaten egg add a tablespoonful of sugar, turn into a cup, and fill up the cup with milk, stirring all together. Set the cup in a basin of hot water, and bake in the oven until just set. Serve from the cup in which it was baked. The custard may be flavored with lemon or vanilla, if desired.

BEAN BROTH

Look over and wash one cupful of beans, and put to cook in plenty of water, replenishing with hot water occasionally, if necessary. Cook slowly until tender, when there should be but little more than a cupful of broth remaining. Drain this off, season with a spoonful of cream, a little salt, and serve hot.

WHITE OF EGG AND MILK

Beat the white of an egg to a stiff froth, and stir briskly into a glass of cold milk. Good for persons with weak digestion.

STEAMED EGG

Break an egg into an egg-cup or patty-pan, sprinkle slightly with salt, and steam over boiling water until the white is set.

SCRAMBLED EGG

Heat two tablespoonfuls of water in a saucepan, break into it a fresh egg, and stir lightly until set, but not stiff. Add salt, and serve on toast.

BAKED MILK

Put the milk into an earthen jar, cover the opening with a white paper, and bake in a moderate oven until thick as cream. May be taken by the most delicate stomach.

TAPIOCA CUP CUSTARD

Soak one tablespoonful of tapioca in a small cup of milk for two hours; then stir in the beaten yolk of a fresh egg, a teaspoonful of sugar, and a very little salt; turn into a cup, and bake in the oven for twelve or fifteen minutes.

Will fortune never come with both hands full,
And write her fair words still in foulest letters?
She either gives a stomach, and no food,—
Such are the poor, in health, or else a feast,
And takes away the stomach,—such are the rich,
That have abundance, and enjoy it not.
—*Shakespeare.*

OATMEAL WATER AND MILK

For an infant under three months, put one tablespoonful of fine oatmeal into a pint of boiling water, boil for an hour, replenishing with boiling water to keep the quantity good; strain, and add one cup of sterilized milk. Feed in bottle. For infants from three to six months, use equal portions of milk and oatmeal water, and after six months, two-thirds milk.

SUBSTITUTE FOR MOTHER’S MILK, NO. 1

Take one ounce cow’s milk, two ounces cream, three drams milk sugar, one grain bicarbonate of soda, and one ounce of water. Increase the quantity of milk and cream as the child gets older.

SUBSTITUTE FOR MOTHER’S MILK, NO. 2

Take one tablespoonful of cream, four of milk, two of limewater, and four of sweetened water. Sugar of milk, two ounces to a pint of water, is preferable to ordinary sugar for preparing the sweetened water. This will generally agree with the most delicate stomach.

WHITE OF EGG AND WATER

Stir well the white of an egg into a cupful of as warm water as can be used without coagulating the egg. Good for infants suffering with extremely weak digestion, and unable to take milk.

TO STERILIZE MILK

As soon as received, heat to nearly the boiling-point; then remove from the fire, and cool as quickly as possible, by pouring it into clean pans, previously scalded, and placing these in cold water.

COTTAGE CHEESE

Set a pan containing a quart or more of thick, sour milk in a pan of hot water, or on the back of the stove; as soon as the whey separates from the curd, line a colander with a cloth, pour in the scalded milk, tie the corners of the cloth together, and hang up till well drained; put into a bowl, add one-fourth teaspoonful of salt, and enough sweet cream to make as moist as desired; mix smooth with a spoon, turn lightly into a dish, and serve.

HOMINY OR HULLED CORN

To hull four quarts of corn, use one heaping tablespoonful of soda, and water enough to cover the corn. Boil for four hours, or until the hull is well loosened and can be readily removed. Then wash in cold water thoroughly, stirring, rubbing, and rinsing until the hulls have all been turned off. Soak in clear water overnight to remove all traces of soda, and cook in a kettle or large saucepan all day in clear water, stirring occasionally to prevent burning on the bottom, and replenishing with hot water as needed. Season with salt, put into a jar, and keep in a cool place.

DRIED SWEET CORN

Remove the husks and silks, boil and cut from the cob as directed for stewed sweet corn on page 57. Spread thinly on a cloth or on shallow tins, and place in the sun to dry. Turn over occasionally, take in in the evening, and put out to dry every day until thoroughly hard and dry. To keep off flies and insects, cover with mosquito webbing. Corn may also be dried in a warm, open oven, if careful not to allow the oven to get too hot. When dry, soak and cook the same as stewed sweet corn, only longer; or with beans soaked overnight.

DRIED APPLES

Take good, ripe apples, pare, quarter, core, and cut into thin slices; spread on shallow tins, and place in the oven until well heated through, then in the sun or in a moderate, open oven until thoroughly dried. Turn the fruit over occasionally each day while drying. Wire screens or webbings are serviceable in keeping off the flies. Other fruits may be dried in a similar manner.

POP-CORN

Shell, and place a handful in a wire popper or frying-pan, covering tightly; shake constantly over a hot fire, being careful not to burn. When the popping ceases, it is done; add a little salt and butter; mix with it a little thick sugar sirup, or molasses boiled down, and press it into balls with the hands slightly oiled.

TO KEEP APPLES, ORANGES, AND LEMONS

Wrap each separately in tissue paper, and lay so as not to touch each other, in a cool, dry place.

TO KEEP EGGS

To twelve quarts of water add two pints of fresh, slaked lime and one pint of common salt; mix well, immerse newly-laid eggs, and set in a cool place. Or, dip the eggs into a solution of gum arabic—equal parts gum and water

—let dry, then dip again. When dry, wrap separately in paper, and pack in sawdust, bran, or salt.

TO PRESERVE LEMON-JUICE

When lemons are cheap, purchase several dozen at once. With the hand press each lemon on the table, rolling it back and forth briskly a few times; cut into halves, and extract the juice with a lemon drill into a bowl or tumbler,—never into a tin; strain the juice through a wire strainer, colander, or coarse cloth to remove the seeds and pulp; add a pint of water and a pound of white sugar to the juice of each dozen lemons, and boil in an enameled saucepan for about ten minutes; then bottle and set in a cool place, and it is ready for use. A tablespoonful or two of the sirup in a glass of water makes a cooling, healthful drink.

COOKED PINEAPPLE

Pare with a sharp knife, cut into thin slices, divide the slices into quarters, put into a saucepan with one-half cup of water, and a very little sugar for each pineapple; cover with a china plate or enameled lid, and cook slowly for about two hours.

TO FROST FRUITS

Secure nice bunches of cherries, currants, grapes, or berries with the stems on; dip them into the stiffly beaten white of an egg, then into powdered sugar, and place on a plate or clean white paper so as not to touch each other, to dry. Then place the fruit on a glass dish, chill, and serve.

UNLEAVENED BREAD FOR SACRAMENTAL USE

Take three cups of white flour, half a cup of thick sweet cream, a pinch of salt, and a little cold water. Sift the flour into a dish, add the salt and cream, and rub together thoroughly; then moisten with cold water till of the consistency of thick pie crust. Knead and roll well with the hand for fifteen minutes; then roll out to about a quarter of an inch in thickness, and cut into cakes four inches square. Mark out each cake into half-inch squares with a knife, so that when baked it may easily be broken, and prick each square with a fork to prevent blistering. Lay on floured baking tins, and bake in a quick oven, being careful not to scorch or burn.

UNFERMENTED WINE FOR SACRAMENTAL USE

Secure good grapes, the small, dark wine grape is preferable, and proceed as with grape juice on page 46.

TO CUT LEMONS FOR GARNISHING

Divide slices of lemons into four parts, and use on salads and other dishes, placing the points toward the center.

HOW TO CUT BREAD

Bread Knife

Bread should be cut into smooth, even slices, not too thick, the full length or width of the loaf. If large, the slices may be divided. The Clauss, or scalloped-edged, bread-knife does the work nicely. If bread or cake is to be cut while warm, the knife should first be heated.

NUT RELISH

Take one cup of almond or peanut butter, one cup of dried figs, or seedless raisins, and one cup of gluten. Mix well together, then grind twice through a nut mill. Mold into a square pan, then cut into inch squares one-half inch thick, similar in size to caramels.

NUT DAINTIES

Crack English walnuts so as not to break the meats. Take the two halves from each nut and press on each side of a nut relish square. When sufficient are prepared, place in a dish with an equal number of olives.

A WEEK'S MENU

FIRST DAY	
Breakfast	
Fresh Fruit	
Oatmeal Mush	Breakfast Rolls
Zwieback	Stewed Fruit
Cereal	Coffee
Dinner	
Split Pea Soup	
Mashed Potatoes with Brown Sauce	
Scalloped Tomatoes Brown Bread	
French Rolls	Baked Apples
Rice Custard	
SECOND DAY	
Breakfast	
Fresh Fruit	
Corn Flakes	
Graham Gems	Whole Wheat Crisps
Egg Toast	Cereal Coffee
Dinner	
Potato Soup	
Boiled Potatoes	Baked Beans
Stewed Cauliflower	
Brown and White Bread	Rusks
Bananas	Pumpkin Pie
THIRD DAY	
Breakfast	
Boiled Rice	
Baked Potatoes	Plain Omelet
Cream Toast	Sticks

Hot Milk	
Dinner	
Bean Soup	
Mashed Potatoes	Stewed Turnips
Brown and White Bread	
Peach Pie	Fruit Biscuit
FOURTH DAY	
Breakfast	
Fresh Apples	Cream of Wheat
Toast with Cream	
Rice Waffles	Stewed Pears
Cereal	Coffee
Dinner	
Lentil Soup	
Baked Sweet Potatoes, Cream Sauce	
Tomato Salad	
Boiled Beans with Rice	
Corn-meal Gems	Sago Pudding
FIFTH DAY	
Breakfast	
Fresh Fruit	
Graham Mush with Dates	
Oatmeal	Gems Baked Sweet Apples
Berry Toast	Cambric Tea
Dinner	
Vegetable Soup	
Potatoes with Cream	Stewed Asparagus
Boiled Sweet Corn	
Brown and White Bread	
Stewed Prunes	Cream Pie
SIXTH DAY	
Breakfast	

Corn-meal Mush	
Rice Cakes	Stewed Fruit
Whole Wheat Bread	Egg Toast
Cereal Coffee or Hot Milk	
Dinner	
Rice Soup	
Mashed Potatoes	Green Peas
Succotash	
Brown and White Bread	
Apple Float	Raised Biscuits
SABBATH	
Breakfast	
Oranges and Bananas	
Graham Mush with Dates	
Stewed Prunes	
Parker House Rolls	
Brown and White Bread	
Cereal	Coffee
Dinner	
Split Pea and Vermicelli Soup	
Baked Beans	
Warmed-up Potatoes	Fruit Buns
Brown and White Bread	
Lemon or Prune Pie	Orangeade
Fresh Fruit and Nuts	

NOTE.—The above is simply suggestive, and may be simplified, enlarged, or varied as desired. It is not supposed that every person shall necessarily eat everything indicated for each meal. Some will prefer the grain and vegetable dishes; others the grain and fruit. If a third meal is eaten, either at middle or close of day, it should be light and simple,—a mere lunch.

SABBATH DINNERS

The Sabbath is the day of rest. In order that it may be devoted by all to religious exercises, holy meditation, and spiritual delight, it should be as free as possible from the ordinary duties and cares of life. To make it thus, preparation on the day before is necessary. The Lord calls the day before the Sabbath "the preparation" day. Luke 23:54. Of the work to be done on this day he says: "To-morrow is the rest of the holy Sabbath unto the Lord: bake that which ye will bake to-day, and seethe [boil] that ye will seethe; and that which remaineth over lay up for you to be kept until the morning." Ex. 16:23.

The Sabbath should not be made a day of feasting. The labor of the week being laid aside, a moderate amount of plain, wholesome food is all that is necessary. To gormandize on this day, as is the custom with many, causes the mind to become dull and stupid, and unfits it for spiritual devotion.

With proper planning, very little, if any, cooking need ever be done on the Sabbath, aside from simply warming over some of the foods prepared the previous day.

Brown bread, fruit bread-sticks, or French rolls; warmed up potatoes, or potatoes with cream; baked or boiled beans; split pea or lentil soup, with croutons; sago, tapioca, or some other simple pudding or pie; canned or stewed fruit; and fresh fruits and nuts, make an excellent Sabbath dinner. All these may be prepared on the previous day. The potatoes may be boiled ready to warm up, the beans baked or boiled, the peas or lentils cooked and rubbed through a colander ready to add the seasoning and necessary water for soup, the croutons prepared, the fruit stewed, the pudding or pie baked, and the nuts cracked. Then the dinner may be made ready quickly, and with but little effort.

FOOD COMBINATIONS

Because of their chemical nature, the time required to digest them, and the place where, and the juices with which, they are digested, some foods do not combine as well as others. While the young and those with sound stomachs and vigorous digestion may experience little or no inconvenience from improper and more varied combinations, to continue their use is likely in time seriously to impair the digestion. Dyspeptics and those troubled with slow digestion will find it to their advantage to avoid such combinations as fruits and vegetables, milk and vegetables, sugar and milk, milk and fruits; and, when fruits are taken, to eat them at the close of the meal. The following are good combinations: Grains and fruits; fruits and nuts; grains, fruits, and nuts; grains, legumes, and vegetables; grains and milk. An excellent rule to follow is to avoid a large variety at any meal, and let natural cravings indicate largely the kinds of food eaten. Above all, use common sense, and relish what you eat.

TIME REQUIRED TO DIGEST VARIOUS FOODS

	Hrs.	Mins.
Rice	1	00
Apples, sweet, mellow, raw	1	00
Granola	1	00
Eggs, whipped	1	30
Trout, boiled	1	30
Venison, broiled	1	35

Sago	1	45
Tapioca	2	00
Barley	2	00
Eggs raw	2	00
Apples, sour, mellow, raw	2	00
Milk, boiled	2	00
Milk, raw	2	15
Turkey, boiled	2	25
Parsnips, boiled	2	30
Potatoes, baked	2	30
Beans, string, boiled	2	30
Cabbage, raw	2	30
Turkey, roasted	2	30
Goose, roasted	2	30
Lamb, boiled	2	30
Oysters, raw	2	55
Eggs, soft boiled	3	00
Beef, lean, raw, roasted	3	00
Beefsteak, broiled	3	00
Chicken soup, boiled	3	00
Mutton, broiled	3	00
Bean soup	3	00
Mutton, roasted	3	15
Bread, corn-meal	3	15
Mutton soup	3	30
Bread, white	3	30
Potatoes, boiled	3	30
Turnips, boiled	3	30
Eggs, hard boiled	3	00
Eggs, fried	3	30
Oysters, stewed	3	30
Butter, melted	3	30

Cheese	3	30
Beets, boiled	3	45
Corn and Beans, green	3	45
Veal, broiled	4	00
Fowl, broiled	4	00
Beef, lean, fried	4	00
Salmon, salted, boiled	4	00
Beef, salted, boiled	4	15
Soup, marrow-bone	4	15
Pork, salted, fried	4	15
Veal, fried	4	30
Duck, roasted	4	30
Cabbage, boiled	4	30
Pork, roasted	5	15

NUTRITIVE VALUE OF FOODS

The nutritive food elements are classified into three groups. The *nitrogenous*, or muscle- and tissue-building; the *carbonaceous*, or heat- and energy-producing; and the *mineral*, or the bone- and nerve-building.

Albumen, gluten, and casein belong to the nitrogenous; starch, sugar, and fats to the carbonaceous; and salts, cellulose portions, and inorganic substances to the mineral.

The nitrogenous elements are of prime importance, as they nourish the brain, nerves, muscles, and the more highly vitalized tissues of the body. The carbonaceous, however, are required in much larger quantities, the correct proportion being about eight or ten of carbonaceous to one of nitrogenous.

FOODS	Nitrogenous	Carbonaceous	Mineral	Total Nutritive Value
GRAINS				
Wheat	10.8	72.5	1.7	85.0
Barley	6.3	76.7	2.0	85.0
Oats	12.6	69.4	3.0	85.0
Rye	8.0	75.2	1.8	85.0
Corn	11.1	73.2	1.7	86.0
Rice	6.3	80.2	0.5	87.0
FRUITS				
Banana	4.8	20.2	0.8	25.8
Date	9.0	58.0	...	67.0
Grape	0.8	14.3	0.3	15.4
Apple	0.2	10.3	0.4	10.9
Pear	0.2	10.2	0.3	10.7
Peach	0.4	7.8	0.4	8.6
Plum	0.2	9.3	0.6	10.1

Cherry	0.9	15.3	0.6	16.8
Blackberry	0.5	5.8	0.4	6.7
Gooseberry	0.4	8.9	0.3	9.6
Raspberry	0.5	6.4	0.5	7.4
Currant	0.4	5.0	0.5	5.9
Apricot	0.5	12.2	0.8	13.5
VEGETABLES				
Arrowroot	...	82.0	...	82.0
Potato	2.1	22.2	0.7	25.0
Sweet Potato	1.5	27.5	2.6	31.6
Carrot	1.3	14.7	1.0	17.0
Beet	1.5	11.3	3.7	16.5
Parsnip	1.1	15.9	1.0	18.0
Cabbage	0.9	4.1	0.6	5.6
Turnip	1.2	7.2	0.6	9.0
LEGUMES				
Peas	23.8	60.8	2.1	86.7
Beans	30.8	50.2	3.5	84.5
Lentils	25.2	58.6	2.3	86.1
NUTS				
Peanut	28.3	48.0	3.3	79.6
Almond	23.5	60.8	3.0	87.3
Cocoanut	5.6	43.9	1.0	50.5
Walnut	15.8	60.4	2.0	88.2
Hazelnut	17.4	60.8	2.5	89.7
SWEETS				
Sugar	...	95.0	...	95.0
Molasses	...	77.0	...	77.0
MILK				
New Milk	4.1	9.1	0.8	14.0
Cream	2.7	29.5	1.8	34.0
Skimmed Milk	4.0	7.2	0.8	12.0

MEATS				
Lean Mutton	18.3	4.9	4.8	28.0
Lean Beef	19.3	3.6	5.1	28.0
Veal	16.5	15.8	4.7	37.0
Pork	9.8	48.9	2.3	61.0
Poultry	21.0	3.8	1.2	26.0
White Fish	18.1	2.9	1.0	22.0
Salmon	16.1	5.5	1.4	23.0
Egg	14.0	10.5	1.5	26.0

NOTE.—From the above it will be seen that grains, legumes, nuts, and sweets, as well as some fruits and vegetables, contain more nourishment than do meats.

HOW TO BECOME A VEGETARIAN

The fact that many people abstain from flesh food altogether, and maintain their full vigor, is good proof that the eating of flesh-meat is not essential to either life or health. But those accustomed all their life to the use of meat may need to use a little caution in making a change to a vegetarian diet. A good way to begin might be to limit one's self at first to the use of meat once or twice a week, discarding it as better foods are substituted. The British Vegetarian Society, in "How to Begin," gives the following suggestions for those desiring to make this change:—

1. *Steadily persevere.*

2. *Use Variety.*—Nature affords the most bountiful abundance. Have something new on your table frequently, especially fruits.

3. *Choose foods which compel mastication.*

4. *Drink Little.*—If fruits be used plentifully—condiments, hot foods, and stimulants avoided, and frequently bathing practised—little drink will be required.

5. *Prefer natural to manufactured foods.*

6. *Avoid Excess.*—Most people eat too much; a smaller quantity of food, well masticated, will nourish and sustain the system best.

7. *Eat Seldom.*—Not more than thrice daily. "Little and often" is an unwise maxim for any healthy person. And if you wish sound sleep, and an appetite for breakfast, avoid suppers.

8. *Let your food be attractively prepared.*

9. *See That Your Life be Right in Other Respects.*—Eat food which is pure of its kind, agreeably prepared, at right times, and in right quantities; breathe pure air by night and by day; take physical exercise (if possible in the open air) daily; and practise strict cleanliness.

10. *Get Mind and Body in Harmony.*—Remember that man's physical condition, and the state of his spiritual and mental faculties are closely and mutually inter-dependent. It is, therefore, a primary essential to keep these also in health; and to see that they be usefully, tranquilly, and constantly occupied and cultivated.

VEGETARIANISM IN LONDON

Vegetarianism has worked an improvement, and its many restaurants in London show how the taste for this diet has been on the increase of late. One very great and undeniable advantage in the teaching of this school is the showing us how many foods we possess, and how few, comparatively speaking, we have used. Also, it proves to us how much cheaper we could live by utilizing all the foods at our command except meat, and abstaining from it.—*Mrs. Beeton.*

RULES FOR DYSPEPTICS

Dyspepsia, or indigestion, is coming to be so general as to demand serious attention. The following rules will be found valuable to those suffering with this complaint:—

1. Eat slowly, chewing the food very thoroughly, even more so, if possible, than is required in health. The more time the food spends in the mouth, the less it will need to spend in the stomach.

2. Avoid drinking at meals; at most, take a few sips of warm drink at the close of the meal, if the food is very dry.

3. In general, dyspeptic stomachs manage dry food better than that containing much fluid.

4. Eat neither very hot nor very cold food. The best temperature is about that of the body. Avoid exposure to cold after eating.

5. Be careful to avoid excess in eating. Eat no more than the wants of the system require. Sometimes less than is really needed must be

taken when the digestion is very weak. Strength depends not on what is eaten, but on what is digested.

6. Never take violent exercise, either mental or physical, just before or just after a meal. Do not go to sleep immediately after eating.

7. Do not eat more than three times a day, and make the last meal very light. For many dyspeptics two meals are better than more.

8. Avoid eating two meals too close together, as this is one of the most prolific causes of indigestion.

9. Observe regularity in eating; do not eat between meals.

10. Never eat when very tired, whether exhausted from mental or physical labor. Rest first.

11. Never eat when the mind is worried, or the temper is ruffled, if possible to avoid doing so.

12. Eat only food that is easy of digestion, avoiding complicated and indigestible dishes, and taking from but one to three kinds at a meal.

13. Omit a meal occasionally, or fast a day. This will give the stomach time to rest and recuperate, and will be found beneficial.

14. If the stomach or bowels feel weak or tender, apply hot fomentations over them.

15. Most persons will be benefited by the use of oatmeal, Graham flour, cracked wheat, whole wheat flour, and other whole-grain preparations, though many will find it necessary to avoid vegetables, especially when fruits are taken.

THE PULSE IN HEALTH

	PER MIN.
At birth	150-130
One month	140-120
Six months	130

One year	120-108
Two years	110-100
Three years	100-90
Seven years	80
Fourteen years	85-80
Adult age	75-70
Old age	65-60

WEIGHTS AND MEASURES FOR THE KITCHEN

3 teaspoonfuls	1 tablespoonful	
16 tablespoonfuls	1 cupful	
2 cupfuls	about	1 pint
4 cupfuls	"	1 quart
2 cupfuls of granulated sugar	"	1 pound
3 cupfuls brown sugar	"	1 pound
2 cupfuls of butter	"	1 pound
2 cupfuls of flour or oatmeal	"	1 pound
4 cupfuls of sifted flour	"	1 pound
1 pint of liquid	"	1 pound
10 eggs	"	1 pound
1 egg	"	2 ounces
1 heaping tablespoonful of sugar	"	1 ounce
2 rounding tablespoonfuls of flour	"	1 ounce
1 tablespoonful of butter	"	1 ounce
5 heaping tablespoonfuls of flour	"	1 cupful
7 heaping tablespoonfuls of sugar	"	1 cupful

HOUSEHOLD HINTS

Every housewife should take pride in keeping her home neat and tidy. "Order is heaven's first law."

Sinks and drains should be frequently cleaned and disinfected.

Dish-cloths should always be washed out after using; otherwise they are liable to become foul and full of germs.

After washing the dishes, pour over them scalding water, and wipe quickly with a clean dry cloth. This insures cleanliness, and gives a nice polish.

Scour steel knives after each meal.

Sweep out the corners, and under the tables and chairs as well as the middle of the room. “Dirt may be hated, but should never be hidden.”

Pare vegetables and fruits thin; study how to use left-over foods; save the bread crumbs for puddings and scalloped vegetables. “Gather up the fragments that remain, that nothing be lost.”

Lightning Source UK Ltd.
Milton Keynes UK
UKHW051126250123
415939UK00013B/519